ENGLISH FOR ACADEMIC STUDY SERIES

WRITING

Student's Book

Ron White and Don McGovern

New York   London   Toronto   Sydney   Tokyo   Singapore

Published 1998 by
Prentice Hall Europe
An imprint of
Pearson Education Limited
Edinburgh Gate
Harlow
Essex CM20 2JE   England

First published 1994 by Prentice Hall International

Typeset in 11/12 Garamond
by Fakenham Photosetting Limited

Printed and bound in Great Britain by
Redwood Books, Trowbridge, Wiltshire

Library of Congress Cataloging in Publication Data

White, Ronald V.
    Writing : student's book / Ron White, Don McGovern.
      p.   cm. – (English for academic study)
    ISBN 0-13-017880-2
    1. English language – Textbooks for foreign speakers.   2. English
language – Rhetoric – Problems, exercises, etc.   I. McGovern, Don,
1949–1993.   II. Title.   III. Series.
PE1125.W718   1994
808'.042 – dc20   94-26133
                                                             CIP

British Library Cataloguing in Publication Data

A catalogue record for this book is available from the British Library

ISBN 0–13–017880–2

---

4 5 6 7 8 03 02 01 00 99

WRITING

STUDENT'S BOOK

Other titles in the English for Academic Study series:

MCGOVERN, D., MATTHEWS, M. and MACKAY, S.
Reading

TRZECIAK, J. and MACKAY, S.
Study Skills for Academic Writing

The English for Academic Purposes series:

ST JOHN YATES, C.
Agriculture

VAUGHAN JAMES, C.
Business Studies

WALKER, T.
Computer Studies

ST JOHN YATES, C.
Earth Sciences

ST JOHN YATES, C.
Economics

JOHNSON, D. and JOHNSON, C. M.
General Engineering

JAMES, D. V.
Medicine

CONTENTS

DEDICATION

This book is dedicated to the memory of Don McGovern (1949–1993) writer and poet, whose imagination, care and profundity in wide-ranging concerns of language and the performing arts won him respect wherever he worked.

His work on this book and the Reading volume in this series was completed shortly before his untimely death.

ACKNOWLEDGEMENTS

The authors and publishers would like to thank the following for permission to reproduce the texts in this book:

The Independent for adaptation of 'The folly of perfection' by Dr. Frans Berkout (1 May 1989) and adaptations of 'Wish you weren't here' by Frank Barrett (15 Aug. 1990).

The Independent on Sunday for adaptations of 'Death by tourism' by David Nicholson-Lord (5 Aug. 1990).

The Independent Magazine for adaptations of 'Pros and cons of tourism' by Roy Jenkins (7 April 1990).

Finance and Development for adaptation of 'Protecting the ozone layer' by Mohan Munasinghe and Kenneth Sing (June 1992).

The Guardian for adaptation of report based on an article in the *Journal of the Air Pollution Control Association* vol. 39:517 (6 Aug. 1989).

Longman for definition in *A First Dictionary of Linguistics and Phonetics* by David Crystal ed. (1980).

INTRODUCING THIS BOOK

A new approach to writing

The approach used in this book will probably be new for you. It is based on academic and scientific research into the mental processes which writers undergo in the stages of composing a written test. This relatively new approach to the teaching of writing, sometimes referred to as *writing as process*, is now widely used on writing courses in the UK and the United States. It has been shown to lead to rapid improvement in the academic writing of learners of English as a second language.

The process approach is based on a number of principles, which can be summarised briefly as follows:

1. Writing is best seen as a recursive process. To put it more simply, you write more effectively by *rewriting* and *revising* at each stage of the composing process – by 'going back' and thinking again and then moving forward.

    Your teacher will ask you to do this in a number of ways. For example, you will be asked to plan your essays and to write at least two drafts rather than one. Furthermore, when you have planned an essay, you will be asked to 'go back' and revise the plan. When the first draft is completed, you will then be asked to revise or edit the first draft before writing a final draft. The result will be a greatly improved essay.

2. The writing process is more satisfying when it is shared and discussed with others at each stage. An open discussion with another writer about problems you may be experiencing, ideas you would like to test, and so on, will help you in many ways as you write.

    For this reason, your teacher will ask you at each stage to discuss your writing with a partner, to offer advice with problems if necessary and to comment on his or her work in a helpful way. Your partner will be asked to do the same for you.

3. Your academic writing will rapidly improve when you try to look at your own writing as a *reader*. To put it another way, your writing will benefit when you become a good critic – a critic of both your own writing and that of other people. This involves evaluation and constructive criticism in which you think about both the strengths and the weaknesses in your writing.

    This book provides a series of questions and sets of guidelines – called evaluation checklists – to help you do this. They can be found on pages 21 and 29 (there are frequent references throughout the book to these checklists and to the five appendices at the end of the book). Your teacher will ask you to evaluate your own writing in a balanced and constructive way so that you can rewrite more effectively. You will then be asked to practise these skills on the writing of another person.

A typical writing task in these units will have the following stages:

- discussion
- brainstorming
- self-evaluation
- planning
- peer evaluation
- writing the first draft
- self-evaluation
- peer evaluation
- revision/rewriting
- writing the second draft
- teacher evaluation and marking.

This approach to writing will take place in an informal 'workshop' atmosphere in the classroom. If you are accustomed to more traditional teaching methods, this may surprise you at first. During a writing task your teacher will circulate and discuss your writing with you in a cooperative way. Do not, however, expect to be given 'the right answers'. Your teacher will often ask you to make your own decisions. The aim of this is to achieve what is sometimes called *learner independence*. This independence will be expected of you during your degree course.

Because of this need for evaluation and revision, the writing of essays will take more time than you are probably used to. Don't worry about this. By your third or fourth essay, you should find that your writing has improved both in *speed* and – more importantly – in *quality*.

Remember that rewriting is not a sign of failure. The most important difference between professional writers and other writers is that professional writers usually rewrite much more than others do.

The last section of this book provides guidelines for further writing to help you apply the process approach to your writing during your degree course.

Integration of Writing and Reading courses

The Writing course can be used on its own or in combination with the Reading course in the *English for Academic Study* series. The seven units in the Writing book have been fully integrated with the seven units in the Reading book. This means that the two books can be treated as one course. The units have been designed in such a way that if you combine the Reading course with the Writing course, you will complete a Reading unit before you move on to the corresponding Writing unit.

The topics in the Reading units are closely related to those in the Writing units. For example, in Reading Unit 2, you will read about some of the problems which overseas students experience when studying in the UK. In Writing Unit 2, you will write an essay defending the value of sending students to study abroad.

You will also find similar points of language use and patterns of organisation in each pair of units. For example, in Reading Unit 4, you will be asked to recognise the patterns of organisation which present a problem and then propose a solution. In Writing Unit 4, you will then be asked to produce this pattern of organisation in an essay on global warming.

In this way there will be a gradual progression from reading to writing, and the information in the Reading texts can be used to help you produce the written material in the corresponding Writing unit.

UNIT 1

WRITING ABOUT WRITING

> ## This unit will ask you to think about:
>
> 1. The nature of academic writing.
>
> 2. The relative importance of different aspects of writing.
>
> 3. The extent to which academic writing can be seen as communicating with another person.
>
> 4. The different stages of the writing process and how they can be approached.
>
> 5. Identifying and coping with difficulties in academic writing.
>
> ## It will then give you practice in:
>
> 1. Writing about academic writing in terms of your views and experience.
>
> 2. Considering the knowledge and expectations of your reader.
>
> 3. Thinking about different approaches to the organisation of your ideas.
>
> 4. Sharing the writing process through:
>
>   • discussion of its different stages with another person
>
>   • exchanging drafts with another person and giving constructive criticism.
>
> 5. Rewriting to correct and improve your first draft.

TASK 1

This task will start you thinking about academic writing. Complete the following questionnaire. You can draw on your experience of writing in your first language and/or in English.

Academic writing: questionnaire

1. What is academic writing? (Please tick ✓ one or more.)

Tick here

	A mechanical exercise
	Sets of grammatically correct sentences
	The clear expression of ideas, knowledge and information
	A form of self-expression
	A way of thinking about academic problems
	Other (please specify)

2. In order to write well academically, how important are the following? (Tick ✓ H for high importance, M for medium importance, L for low importance.)

H	M	L	
			Reading widely and frequently
			Studying grammar
			Studying vocabulary
			Imitating other writers
			Writing frequently
			Inviting others to comment on your writing
			Going back and thinking again about what you are writing
			Rewriting repeatedly until you are satisfied

3. How important do you think the following are? (Tick ✓ H for high importance, M for medium importance, L for low importance.)

H	M	L	
			Grammatical correctness
			Punctuation
			Subject content
			Spelling
			Overall organisation
			Vocabulary
			Good ideas

4. Should you always think of writing as communicating with another person? Why?/Why not?

_____   _____
_____   _____
_____   _____
_____   _____

5. When you write something important, do you write more than one draft?   Yes/No

6. What do you do or what do you concentrate on when you have to write something for someone else to read?

(a) Before you start writing

_____   _____
_____   _____
_____   _____

(b) While you are writing your first draft (this assumes that you write more than one draft)

_____   _____
_____   _____
_____   _____
_____   _____

(c) When you have finished your first draft

_____   _____
_____   _____
_____   _____
_____   _____

(d) Before you 'publish' your final draft by giving or sending it to the intended reader

_____   _____
_____   _____
_____   _____
_____   _____

7. What difficulties do you have with writing? What kind of writing do you have difficulties with?

_____   _____
_____   _____
_____   _____
_____   _____

8. What do you do when you have difficulties? For example, do you put the writing aside and come back to it later, do you ask someone for help, do you refer to notes or other printed sources, do you refer to a text book?

_____   _____
_____   _____
_____   _____
_____   _____

9. How does your usual approach to writing compare with the process approach described in the introduction to this book?

_____   _____
_____   _____
_____   _____
_____   _____

10. What do you enjoy about writing?

_____   _____
_____   _____
_____   _____
_____   _____

When you have finished the questionnaire, compare your answers with those of other people in your group. Combine the answers in one group version of the questionnaire. Do you find that you all have very similar views and experience? Or are your views and experience very different? Are there any general trends among the group?

In the next task, you will draft a report based on the questionnaire and your discussion.

TASK 2

The essay you will prepare in this unit is on the following topic:

> **Academic writing: my views and experience**

This essay is for your teacher. Before you begin writing, discuss in your group the following points:

- What do you think your teacher will want to know about the writing experience of individuals in your class?
- Why do you think he or she wants to know these things?

You can organise your essay in a number of different ways. For example:

- You can follow the order of the questions in the questionnaire.
- You can follow the order of your own life: first learning to read and write in your own language, learning to write in English, writing in your job or profession, and so on.
- You can begin with your greatest problems as a writer and then say how you deal with these problems. For instance, how do you try to meet the needs of your readers?
- You can write about a really important piece of academic writing you have had to do. You can discuss how you did it. You can also relate this to the other kinds of writing you have to do.

You can probably think of other ways of organising your essay too. You should aim to write about 500 words.

 ## Step 1

2.1 When you have decided how you will approach the essay, try brainstorming. In about five minutes write down as many ideas as you can think of on the topic. Don't worry about the order of your ideas at this stage. The important thing is to achieve a rapid and spontaneous 'flow' of ideas in writing. Use rough notes rather than complete sentences.

2.2 Then try to plan your essay by arranging your ideas in a more logical order. You may want to develop some ideas further. You may also want to add a new idea or remove one that is less important. Remember:

- Group ideas together which seem to belong in the same paragraph.
- Think carefully about the order in which you will arrange the paragraphs.

You may want to number the points or use arrows to connect them as you think about the best order for your ideas. Don't worry if you find yourself revising this order more than once.

2.3 Discuss your plan with a partner. When you look at your partner's plan, ask yourself:

- What is the overall idea in the essay?
- Does the plan follow a logical sequence of ideas?
- Are the ideas grouped effectively into paragraphs?
- Is the main idea clear in each paragraph?
- How many paragraphs will the essay contain?

If the answers to these questions are not clear from looking at your partner's plan, ask him or her to explain. Perhaps the plan needs to be changed or developed more fully.

2.4 Think about your partner's comments on your plan and try to improve it.

2.5 Begin writing.

 Step 2

2.6 When you have finished your first draft, find someone else who has also finished. Exchange drafts.

2.7 Read your partner's draft carefully. What are its strengths? What are its weaknesses? Ask yourself whether the writer needs to:

- add information to make things clearer
- remove unnecessary information
- improve the organisation – change the order of ideas, regroup points, etc.
- change the paragraphs – break long paragraphs into shorter ones or combine short paragraphs into a longer one
- join some of the sentences that seem too short
- break some of the long sentences into shorter ones
- improve the use of language – there may be grammatical mistakes
- improve the choice of vocabulary.

2.8 Discuss each other's drafts. Try to comment on both the strengths and weaknesses in your partner's draft. Refer to the points in 2.7 above. Ask each other questions like these:

- Why did you begin as you did?
- Why did you organise the ideas the way you did?
- What is the most important idea in your draft?
- What do you mean by this point? Can you make it clearer?

If points are not clear, or if the writer's main ideas are not clear, discuss these and suggest ways of making them clearer.

2.9 Consider your partner's comments carefully. Which comments do you agree with? Why? Which comments do you disagree with? Why?

 Step 3

2.10 Rewrite your draft, incorporating all the improvements you have discussed and considered in Step 2.

2.11 Check your dictionary for spelling.

Discussion

If you are using the Reading book in this series, you will have read in Unit 1 texts involving educational theory about the need for students to maintain independence and critical judgement in their approach to learning. How do these ideas relate to the work you have done in this unit?

UNIT 2

STUDYING ABROAD

This unit will give you practice in:

1. Understanding different forms of argument.

2. Distinguishing evidence and fact from opinion.

3. Identifying cause and effect relationships and the appropriate markers.

4. Distinguishing between personal and academic style.

5. Writing an essay of argument in the form of a letter to the editor of a newspaper.

6. Evaluating and improving the organisation of your writing through discussion with another person.

7. Evaluating your first draft and another person's first draft with the aid of post-writing questions and an evaluation checklist.

8. Rewriting and improving your draft.

9. Composing a group letter which will contain the best ideas and expressions from a number of second drafts.

TASK 1

 Step 1

1.1 Give three possible meanings of the word *argument*.

1.2 Successful arguing depends on being able to provide evidence in support of your argument. Evidence consists of facts or information giving proof of something.

   Evidence can be contrasted with opinion. The difference may be clear from these examples:

Fact	Opinion
Queen Elizabeth II is a constitutional monarch.	Queen Elizabeth is a kind and hard-working monarch.
Twenty per cent of students at the university are from overseas.	There are too many overseas students at the university.

1.3 Working with a partner, think of two more facts about education, and contrast them with opinions about these facts. Then discuss your facts and opinions with other people in the class.

 Step 2

Reading Unit 2 contains an article about the problems which overseas students can have in adapting to studying and living in the UK.

1.4 Read Text 2.1, which presents another point of view on this topic. It was published in the letters to the editor section of an English-language newspaper in a country in which English is used as a second language.

Text 2.1

Dear Sir,

Many of our best students are going abroad nowadays to study. Why do they go? We have very good universities and colleges in our own country. Our teachers know our local situation, and so what they teach is relevant to local problems.

When our students go abroad, they meet many problems. They find that their teachers know nothing about the countries from which they come. As a result our students learn a lot of useless information. Sometimes they are confused because the foreign teachers tell them things which are different from what they learned at home.

Our students have to study in a foreign language. Therefore they have language problems. What good is studying in English if they are going to work in their own language when they come back?

There is also the question of cost. It is very expensive to send a student to study abroad. Because of this our government has less money to spend on education at home. In my opinion, it would be better to spend the money on improving our own colleges and universities.

Finally, our students come back with many immoral ideas. For this reason studying abroad is corrupting our culture and way of life. I think this is disastrous. So, I believe that students should stay at home to study and not go abroad.

Yours faithfully,
(Name and address supplied)

1.5 How has the writer organised this letter? Identify the main idea in each paragraph and write it in the appropriate space in the following box.

Paragraph	Main idea
1.	
2.	
3.	
4.	
5.	

1.6 How many facts does the writer give? Make a list.

1.7 How many opinions does the writer give? Make a list.

 Step 3

The writer of the letter in Text 2.1 makes a number of cause and effect statements.

1.8 Write an example of a sentence expressing a cause and effect relationship. Here is an example:

> *Because international students are under many pressures, they may suffer from stress related illnesses.*

1.9 There are several English words and phrases which are commonly used to indicate cause and effect relationships. These are called *cause and effect markers*. Make a list of as many as you can think of.

1.10 The writer of the letter in Text 2.1 either expresses or implies a number of cause and effect relationships. Find at least *five* cause and effect relationships in the text. Indicate in each case which word or phrase has been used by the writer as a cause and effect marker.

1.11 Can you find one example of a cause and effect relationship in which these markers are *not* used?

1.12 What evidence is used to support any of the cause and effect relationships which the writer makes?

TASK 2

 Step 1

The writer of Text 2.1. uses a *personal* style, showing the reader that he or she believes in the ideas contained in this letter. The writer is committed to the argument and tries to convince the reader of the strength and importance of these views.

Text 2.2. is an *impersonal* version of the same letter. This time, an objective, academic style is used.

2.1 Read Text 2.2. Identify five differences in style between Text 2.2 and Text 2.1.

Text 2.2

Dear Sir,

Nowadays a large number of this country's best students go abroad to study, even though there are perfectly adequate local institutions of higher education. Furthermore, local faculty are familiar with conditions in this country so that their instruction is relevant to the local situation.

This is to be contrasted with the situation encountered abroad, where faculty tend to be ignorant of their students' countries of origin. As a result, students from this country receive irrelevant instruction which can lead to confusion, particularly when it contradicts what they have already learned.

Another problem faced by this country's students is having to study in a foreign language. There is some doubt about the value and efficiency of studying in another language when, on return to this country, students have to work in their own language. If, instead of going abroad, they studied in this country, such a problem would not arise.

Financially, study overseas is a drain on the economy, reducing the amount available for education in this country. It would be better if the sums spent on higher education abroad could be devoted to the development of local universities and colleges.

Finally, study overseas has a corrupting effect on this country's culture and way of life, since students return with ideas which are out of keeping with local values. For all of the above reasons, priority should be given to studying in this country.

Yours faithfully
(Name and address supplied)

2.2 Does Text 2.2. contain more facts that Text 2.1?

2.3 Choose one of the paragraphs from Texts 2.1 and 2.2. for careful study. Working with a partner, make a list of the differences between the two versions. Here is an example from paragraph 1:

Text 2.1	Text 2.2
Why do they go? (question)	A large number of this country's best students go abroad to study (statement)
our best students	this country's best students
teachers know our local situation	local faculty are familiar with conditions in this country
what they teach is relevant to local problems	their instruction is relevant to the local situation

Draw up a similar table, listing the personal features which appear in your chosen paragraph in the left-hand column under Text 2.1, and the impersonal features in the right-hand column under Text 2.2. Select specific words and phrases as in the example above.

2.4 Discuss the following questions in a group.

- Which version of the letter is more convincing? Why?
- Which version is more authoritative? Why?
- Which version would be more effective for a general readership?
- Which version would be more effective for a professional or academic readership?

TASK 3

In this task you will write a reply to the letter, arguing in favour of studying abroad. To do this you will need to state the case against each of the writer's arguments. Your letter will be published in the same newspaper in the form of a letter to the editor. It should be about 500 to 600 words in length.

You should try to give evidence to support your argument. You can refer to the texts in Reading Unit 2 for some of your evidence if you wish. You may also wish to refer to other sources of evidence.

Think carefully about the use of cause and effect relationships and try to disprove or argue against the cause and effect relationships in the original letter.

You may also wish to propose other cause and effect relationships to support your argument. Make sure that these are clearly indicated.

 Step 1

When you organise your reply, refer back to your analysis of the writer's organisation of ideas in 1.5.

Take care with paragraphing. In general, each paragraph should contain one main point and the main point should be clear to your reader. Each of your paragraphs can follow this pattern:

- State the main idea.
- Discuss the idea, giving examples and evidence.
- Conclude.

3.1 Write down your ideas in note form as quickly as you can, in any order. As in Unit 1, try to achieve a rapid and easy flow of ideas using the brainstorming method.

3.2 Plan your letter by thinking about the order and grouping of your ideas.

- Try to arrange your ideas in a more logical order.
- Decide how your points can be grouped together, so that each group has one main or unifying idea.
- Decide on the most effective order for your groups of points.
- Add notes about further information or ideas which might be necessary to support your main ideas.

3.3 Find a partner and exchange plans. When you read your partner's plan, ask yourself:

- Is the order of points effective?
- Will each group of points form a well-organised paragraph?
- Is the order of groups of points – i.e. paragraphs – effective?
- Do the points follow the order of the original letter? If not, is the new order better?

Discuss your ideas with your partner.

3.4 Think about your partner's comments. Do you agree with them? Try to improve your plan.

 Step 2

3.5 Write your first draft. Try to be authoritative by using an impersonal, academic style, as in Text 2.2. Begin your draft like this:

In reply to the anonymous correspondent who criticised study abroad, I would like to make the following points.

3.6 When you have written your first draft, ask yourself these post-writing questions about the content of your essay. Imagine you are someone else reading the draft for the first time.

- What are the writer's main arguments?
- What evidence does the writer give?
- Is additional information needed?
- Should any information be removed?

3.7 Make improvements to your draft.

 Step 3

3.8 Find a partner and read your drafts aloud to each other.

3.9 Together, work on each other's drafts. Apply the post-writing questions in 3.6 to your partner's draft.

3.10 Refer to Sections 2 and 4 of Evaluation Checklist A at the end of this unit. These sections contain further questions about purpose and organisation which will help you improve both your own and your partner's writing.

3.11 Make written comments and suggestions for improvement on your partner's draft or on another piece of paper. Refer specifically to many of the post-writing questions and the points in Sections 2 and 4 of Evaluation Checklist A. Add your name or initials to these comments when you make them.

3.12 Discuss your comments and suggestions with your partner. Think critically about your partner's comments. Which comments do you agree with? Why? Which comments do you disagree with? Why? Try to be specific in answering these questions.

 Step 4

3.13 To help you make further improvements to your own draft, refer to the list of cause and effect markers in Appendix 1 and to Sections 5 and 6 of Evaluation Checklist A. Think about the cohesion necessary to join your ideas together. Also think about the likely responses of the person who will eventually read your essay.

3.14 Rewrite your draft, with corrections and improvements, and give it to your teacher.

TASK 4

You have now written your first and second drafts. The second draft should be better than the first. Now you are going to write a third draft. This will take the form of a group letter, containing the best ideas and expressions from all of the second drafts in your group.

 Step 1

4.1 Read each other's second drafts (you will have to work quickly). When you read each draft, make a note of one interesting idea which you think should go into the group letter. It can be in the form of a word, phrase or sentence.

4.2 Pass your own draft to the person sitting on your right.

4.3 Read through the draft of the person sitting on your left. When you have read it, pass it on to the person sitting on your right. Continue doing this until your own draft has come back to you.

Step 2

4.4 Nominate a group coordinator who will write down the group's ideas and coordinate the writing of a group letter.

4.5 Choose two ideas which you think should be included in the group letter – one from your own draft and one from somebody else's draft. Give these two ideas to the group coordinator.

　　 Add one other idea from your notes if it seems important and has not already been mentioned.

4.6 Work as a group to collect together similar ideas. You can do this by gathering together ideas under headings such as 'Coping with language problems'.

4.7 Has a common or unifying idea emerged? If there is one common idea, this can be called the *thesis* of your letter. Try to make this clear in the first paragraph of the letter.

4.8 Decide together on the most effective order for the group's main ideas. Consider the order of main ideas in the original letter.

4.9 Think about your readership:

- Who will read your letter first?
- Who will read your letter after it is published?
- What will be the beliefs and attitudes of your readers?
- What is the purpose of your letter in relation to these beliefs and attitudes?

 Step 3

4.10 Discuss as a group how to begin the letter. Think of what you should tell your readers first.

4.11 Begin writing. One possible approach is to give each person in the group one paragraph to write – the conclusion can be written later. The coordinator can then copy or assemble these paragraphs when they are finished.

4.12 Discuss as a group how you will end your letter. Your readers will want you to give a clear and convincing conclusion. If your letter has a thesis, you can return to it in your conclusion.

4.13 Finalise your group letter and give it to your teacher.

Evaluation Checklist A

1. Main idea

What is the writer's overall idea?

2. Writer's purpose

2.1 Is the writer's primary purpose clear? Is the purpose to:
- inform?
- persuade?
- or both?

2.2 Does the writer show how strongly he or she believes in the ideas in the essay? Are the opinions supported with evidence?

3. Content

3.1 Has enough been written about the subject to cover the topic or question adequately?

3.2 Is all the information relevant to the topic?

3.3 Are the main ideas supported by specific examples or evidence?

3.4 Are there any gaps in the information?

3.5 Is there too much information on some points?

4. Structure of text

4.1 Is there a clear introduction and a clear conclusion?

4.2 Is the sequence of ideas clear – earlier to later, general to particular, thesis to supporting points, supporting points to conclusion, weaker arguments to stronger arguments? If not, would it help to rearrange the order of ideas?

4.3 Paragraphs
- (a) Does the text have clear paragraph divisions?
- (b) Is each paragraph built around one main idea or topic?
- (c) Do the paragraph divisions match the organisation of ideas in the plan?

- (d) If not, should any of the paragraphs be:
  - joined together?
  - divided into smaller units?
  - rearranged?

5. Cohesion

(See Appendices 1 and 2.)

5.1 Do the connections between the ideas need to be made more clear or explicit?

5.2 If connecting words like the ones below have been used, have they been used appropriately? Do they give the reader a sense of 'flow' in the writer's ideas? Or do the ideas simply read like a list?

Types of connectors

'And' type: *therefore, as a result, accordingly, consequently, thus*

'Or' type: *in other words, to put it more simply*

'But' type: *however, yet, nevertheless*

Other connectors include:
- *who*
- *which*
- *that*
- *when*
- *where*
- *because*
- *since*
- *although*

(See Appendices 1 and 2 for a full list of cause and effect markers.)

5.3 Use of reference items – words such as *it, they, this, these, those*
- (a) Is each reference item used clearly? Can you easily identify the word or phrase which each one refers to?
- (b) Is each reference item used appropriately

6. Response as readers

6.1 Does the opening paragraph make you want to read on?

6.2 Do you feel satisfied with the way the text comes to an end?

6.3 Indicate your interest in the text as a whole, using a scale from 1 to 5 where 1 is very interesting and 5 is not interesting.

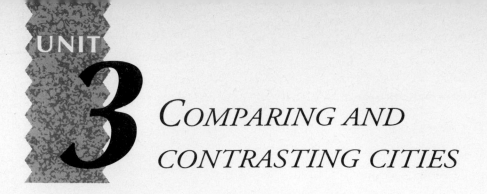

UNIT 3

COMPARING AND CONTRASTING CITIES

> **This unit will give you practice in:**
>
> 1. Understanding how descriptions based on comparison and contrast can be organised.
>
> 2. Recognising words, phrases and structures commonly used in comparison and contrast.
>
> 3. Categorising similarities and differences between two towns or cities.
>
> 4. Writing a description based on comparison and contrast of two towns or cities.
>
> 5. Choosing an audience for your writing and considering their needs.
>
> 6. Asking pre-writing questions about your own knowledge of the subject and your reader's knowledge and attitude.
>
> 7. Asking post-writing questions about the organisation, information and interest of your first draft.
>
> 8. Evaluating your own and another person's draft with the aid of a checklist.

TASK 1

A description based on comparison and contrast can be developed in two ways:

1. You can group the main ideas about Subject A in one paragraph or section and the main ideas about Subject B in the next paragraph or section, in a 'vertical' movement, as in the first of the following diagrams.

2. Alternatively, you can treat the corresponding ideas on Subject A and Subject B as a pair and compare or contrast them one after the other, in a 'horizontal' movement, as in the second diagram.

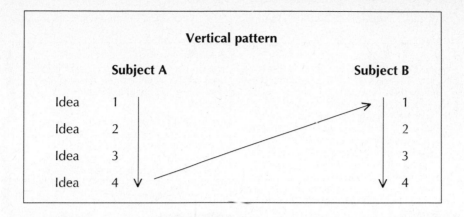

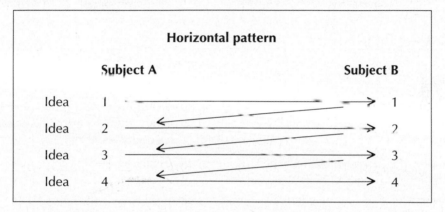

Whether you choose the 'vertical' or the 'horizontal' pattern depends on the kind of text you are writing, its purpose and your own preference. Some writers and readers find the 'horizontal' pattern clearer because it repeatedly reminds them of the comparison or contrast relationship. Others prefer the 'vertical' pattern because of its relative simplicity. The 'horizontal' pattern is often more suitable for a longer piece of writing. Both patterns are commonly used in descriptions involving comparison and contrast.

 Step 1

1.1 Read Text 3.1.

1.2 Consider the following questions:

(a) Is the writer's description based on comparison or contrast – or both?
(b) Has the writer used a 'vertical' or 'horizontal' pattern of organisation?
(c) Which words are used to indicate a relationship of comparison or contrast? Can you think of similar words or phrases? (See Appendix 1.)

> ## Text 3.1
>
> (1) Concepts for the disposal of highly radioactive wastes have been around for more than 40 years. (2) The most authoritative early work was a 1957 report by the US National Academy of Sciences. (3) This recommended that rock-salt would be the most suitable medium in which to emplace wastes because it represented a dry geological environment. (4) In countries with large salt deposits, such as West Germany and the US, the concept of a 'dry' repository took hold. (5) Furthermore, this was the basis of research into disposal until the late 1970s.
>
> (6) In other European countries, however, large salt domes do not exist. (7) From the mid-seventies, having ignored the disposal problem for about two decades, these countries chose instead to look at crystalline rock-types. (8) Invariably these were water-bearing.
>
> Adapted from 'The folly of perfection' by Dr Frans Berkhout, *The Independent*, 1 May 1989

 Step 2

1.3 Rewrite Text 3.1 so that it follows the *opposite* pattern of organisation. In other words, arrange the eight sentences in a new order so that they compare and contrast the subject in a different way. Make any changes that are necessary to:

   • alter the pattern of organisation (this may mean that you will need to make changes to the wording of sentences)

   • mark or signal comparison and contrast relationships with the appropriate words

   • clarify or replace reference items (*it, they, this, these, those*, etc).

Note: Except for these changes, there is no need to alter the wording of the sentences.

1.4 Compare your draft with a partner's draft. Do you agree? Suggest corrections and improvements. (See Appendix 2 for words, phrases and structures commonly used in descriptions involving comparison and contrast.)

TASK 2

 Step 1

2.1 Think of two cities which interest you – they could be two cities in your own country, or a city in your own country and one of a comparable size in another country.

1. List at least three things which are the same or similar about these two cities.
2. List at least three things which are different.

2.2 In a group, compare the answers you have given to each question. Which things did you compare and contrast? Did they include things like location, population and industries?

 Step 2

2.3 Work together to make a list of relevant headings for your points of similarity and difference, such as 'Location' or 'Population'. Group the points you listed in 2.1. under the appropriate headings or categories. For example, under which heading would you put the following points about Reading, a town in England?

- distribution and administration
- in the Thames valley
- about 200,000 people
- 40 miles west of London
- Digital, Hewlett Packard, Porsche UK

This is called *categorising* – in other words, organising information into groups, classes or categories according to similarities and differences.

The heading is sometimes called a *category, characteristic* or *criterion* (plural *criteria*). There are many forms of diagrams that can help you organise information in this way. Two examples are shown below. The diagram on the right is called a *classification diagram.*

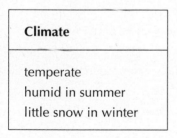
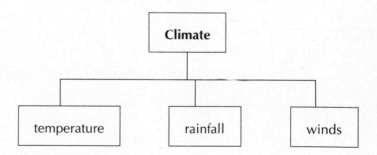

2.4 Now try to think of more points of similarity and difference between your two cities and place them under an appropriate heading.

2.5 Discuss what other headings – or categories – you have not included and add them to your list. For instance, do you have 'Cultural life' as one of your headings? Or 'Entertainment'?

2.6 Make a complete list of all of the main categories or headings that you have listed. Compare your headings with those of another person in your group.

Step 3

2.7 Now draw up a table like the one below. Several categories have been given as examples – you should fill in the table with your own categories as listed in 2.6.

Category	City A	City B
Location		
Population		
Industries		

2.8 Against each of the categories, make a note in your table of specific points relating to City A and to City B.

If you don't have some of the information you need, ask other students in your group or refer to your teacher, who will suggest how you can find out what you need to know. Possible sources of information include:

- a travel book or reference book
- tourist information brochures
- information from travel agents or embassies.

2.9 When you have completed your table, you will have the basis for a comparison of the two cities chosen. Now ask yourself:

- Who (apart from your teacher) would want to read such a comparison?
- Why would they want to read it?
- What would they hope to learn from it?

2.10 Discuss these questions with a partner.

TASK 3

You are now going to write an essay in which you will compare and contrast the two cities you have chosen. An appropriate length would be about 500 words.

If you are using the Reading book, you may want to look at Unit 3 which contains texts on urban development.

Step 1

3.1 Discuss:

- Who are you going to write for? In other words, what is your audience?
- Will your audience be in your own country or in another country?
- In what form do you want your essay to be published or distributed:
  – as an article in a book about your country?
  – as part of an information leaflet for tourists?
  – as part of a university brochure for prospective students?
- Why are you writing? What is your purpose? Do you wish simply to inform the reader? Do you want to convince the reader of the qualities of your town? Do you want to argue about an issue concerned with urbanisation?
- What is the central or main idea that you want to communicate about the subject? In other words, what is your thesis?

3.2 When you have discussed these five questions, write down your answers to each of them.

3.3 Think about the pre-writing questions below before you begin writing your first draft:

- What do I know about these two cities? What do I not know?
- What does my audience already know about these cities? Can I assume that they are familiar with one of them? Both of them?
- What will my readers probably want to know about these cities?
- Will my readers be more interested in one city than the other? What will my readers want to learn from my comparison of the two places?
- What will probably be my readers' attitude towards the subject? If my readers are not likely to be interested, how can I stimulate their interest in reading my comparison?

Discuss these questions with a partner, comparing ways in which you intend to deal with these points, and make notes on your discussion.

 Step 2

3.4 Look again at the table you made in 2.7 and 2.8. Develop this further into a plan for your essay. As you plan your essay, consider the following questions:

- Do I need more/fewer headings or main ideas for my essay?
- Are more/fewer points needed to support and develop any of these headings or main ideas?
- Are these headings or main ideas listed in the most effective order?

- Will I follow a vertical or horizontal pattern of organisation?
- What will be my thesis or overall idea?

3.5 Exchange your plan with a partner. Evaluate the strengths and weaknesses of your partner's plan. Use the questions in 3.4 to help you. Make written comments either on the plan itself or on another piece of paper. Discuss your comments with each other.

3.6 Think critically about your partner's comments. Which comments do you agree with? Why? Which comments do you disagree with? Why? Try to improve your plan.

 Step 3

3.7 Before you write, consider how you could combine your ideas, using some of the markers of comparison and contrast in Appendix 2.

3.8 Write your first draft.

3.9 When you have finished your first draft, read it through and ask yourself the following post-writing questions:

- Have I begun in an interesting way?
- Have I made my thesis or overall idea clear?
- Do I give my readers enough information about both cities? Do I give too much information?
- Is there a balance of information on each city which relates to my readers' interests? If not, how can this be improved?
- Have I written an effective conclusion?
- Have I used either the vertical or horizontal pattern of organisation consistently in my essay?
- Have I used appropriate and effective ways of showing contrast and comparison? (See Appendix 2 for guidance.)

 Step 4

3.10 Read your draft aloud to a partner if you feel it will help to improve what you have written.

3.11 Together, work on each other's drafts. Apply the post-writing questions in 3.9 to each other's drafts.

3.12 Refer to Sections 2 and 3 of Evaluation Checklist B at the end of this unit. These sections will provide further questions about organisation and cohesion which you can apply to both your own writing and your partner's writing. Look at the lists of markers in Appendices 1 and 2 and decide which ones are appropriate to your needs.

3.13 Make written comments and suggestions for improvement on your partner's draft or on another piece of paper. Refer specifically to many of the post-writing questions and the points in Sections 2 and 3 of Evaluation Checklist B. Add your name or initials to these comments when you make them.

3.14 Discuss your comments and suggestions with your partner. Think critically about your partner's comments. Which comments do you agree with? Why? Which comments do you disagree with? Why? Try to be specific in answering these questions.

 Step 5

3.15 Refer to Sections 4 and 6 of Evaluation Checklist B to help you make further improvements to your own draft. These sections deal with vocabulary and mechanical accuracy

3.16 Rewrite your draft, with corrections and improvements, and give it to your teacher.

Evaluation Checklist B

1. Content

1.1 Is all the information relevant to the topic? Is some of it not relevant?

1.2 Are there any gaps in the information?

1.3 Has enough been written about the subject to cover the topic or question adequately?

2. Organisation

2.1 Is the subject or topic stated clearly in the introduction?

2.2 Are the topics or main ideas in each paragraph clear?
- Are there appropriate examples for each main idea?
- Is there enough discussion and analysis of examples?
- Is each paragraph given enough development?

2.3 Does each paragraph 'flow' smoothly, or does it read like a list?

2.4 Is there a conclusion? Does it summarise the main points effectively?

2.5 Could you easily make an outline or diagram of the main ideas after reading this draft?

3. Cohesion

3.1 How do sentences connect with those that come before and those that follow? Are they joined smoothly, or do they read like a list? Do some sentences need to be combined? Do some sentences need to be divided?

3.2 Have enough connectives been used? Have too many connectives been used?
- 'And' type – *therefore, as a result, accordingly*, etc.
  'Or' type – *in other words, to put it more simply*, etc.
  'But' type – *however, yet, nevertheless*, etc.

- Other connectives, such as:
  who, which, that, when, where, because, since, although, etc.

4. Vocabulary

4.1 Is specialist or technical vocabulary accurately used?
  - If written for a general audience, is each term clearly explained when it first occurs?

4.2 Is general vocabulary accurately used?
  - Have words been chosen with an accurate sense of their meaning as well as their use in this context? Can you think of better synonyms for some words?

4.3 Is the writing in a consistently formal style?

5. Grammar

5.1 Do subjects and verbs agree – are singular and plural subjects used with the correct verb forms?
  - Is *s* or *es* used at the end of the third person singular, present simple tense (stem + *s* or *es*)?

5.2 Sometimes *it* or *there* are needed as an impersonal subject. Has either of these words been omitted from an impersonal construction? Example:

  There are many reasons for this conclusion.
  It has been shown that this is not always the case.

5.3 Verb tenses
  - Are verb tenses correctly formed and correctly used?
  - Are the present simple and present continuous used correctly? Is the present continuous used too often?
  - Are the simple past (often used with an adverb of time) and the present perfect used correctly?
  - Are present passive verbs formed correctly? Are passive verbs in the simple past formed correctly? Is the auxiliary verb present (e.g. *is/are, was/were*)?
  - Are too many passive verb forms

used – is the passive used where it is not needed?
  - Are the past tenses of irregular verbs formed correctly?

5.4 Check that the following are correct:
  - Differences between *other* and *another*.
  - Is *this* used with a singular noun and *these* with a plural noun?
  - Are countable and uncountable nouns used correctly?
  - Differences between the negatives *no* and *not*.
  - Are the comparatives and superlatives of adjectives and adverbs formed and used correctly?

5.5 Check the correct use of:
  - Prepositions – *in, on, at, for, to,* etc.
  - Articles – *a, an, the*
  - Relative pronouns – *who, which, that*
  - Possessive adjectives – *his, her, their, its*

6. Mechanical accuracy

6.1 Punctuation
  - Does each sentence end with an appropriate mark of punctuation?
    . full-stop   ? question mark
    ! exclamation mark
  - Is punctuation correctly used within sentences?
    , comma
    ; : semi-colon   colon
    – ( ) dash   brackets (or parentheses)
    ' ' / " " inverted commas/ quotation marks
    ' apostrophe for possessive *s* ('s or *s*')

6.2 Capital letters
  - Are capital letters used where they are needed? Are they used where they are *not* needed?

6.3 Spelling
  - Check the spelling of words that you are not sure about in a dictionary, or use the spelling checker if you are working on a word processor.

UNIT 4

GLOBAL WARMING

This unit will give you practice in:

1. Interpreting data from tables, graphs and diagrams.

2. Recognising and analysing a **Situation→Problem→Solution→Evaluation** pattern in writing.

3. Reorganising a text to follow this pattern.

4. Writing an article on global warming which is organised according to this pattern.

5. Asking pre-writing and post-writing questions about your own and your partner's draft.

6. Evaluating your own draft and another person's draft with the aid of a checklist.

7. Rewriting and improving your draft.

TASK 1

Step 1

1.1 Discuss the problem of global warming:

- What are the causes of global warming?
- What problems will global warming lead to?
- What are possible solutions to these problems?

1.2 Figures 1 to 3 give information about the 'greenhouse' gases which contribute to global warming. Use them to answer the questions which follow and specify which figure your information comes from.

Figure 1: Contribution of greenhouse gases to climate change

Gas and sources	1990 emissions, millions of tonnes	Present concentration in atmosphere	Cut in emissions needed to stabilise concentration	Annual increase in concentration	Global warming potential*
CARBON DIOXIDE: burning fossil fuels and forests, cement making	26,000	354 parts per million in atmosphere	60%–80%	0.5%	1
METHANE: rubbish dumps paddy fields, cattle, tarmac, coal mining, gas leaks	300	1.72 ppm	15%–20%	0.9%	21
CFCs, HCFCs: coolants for fridges, air conditioners, foam-blowing agents, electronics, solvents, aerosols	1	0.001 ppm	70%–85%	4%	6,000
NITROUS OXIDE: burning fossil fuels and forest, fertilisers	6	0.31 ppm	70%–80%	0.25%	290

* A measure of how much warming one tonne of the gas causes over a century, relative to one tonne of carbon dioxide

Figure 2: Greenhouse gases and sea levels

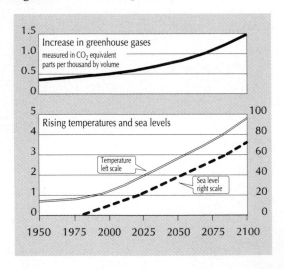

Figure 3: Sources of gases

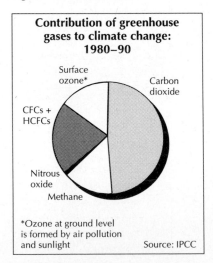

1. Which gas has the highest emission figure?
2. Which gas contributes most to climate change?
3. Which gases have the highest global warming potential?
4. Which gases have the highest rate of annual increase in concentration?

5. What are the main sources of CFCs?
6. What are the main sources of carbon dioxide?
7. By how much is the sea level expected to rise by the year 2050?
8. Which sources of greenhouse gases are easiest to reduce and control?

1.3 Discuss in your group the possible economic and social effects of trying to reduce the emission rates of these greenhouse gases.

 Step 2

1.4 The following pattern of organisation is often found in texts which present problems and explore what can be done about them:

- Situation
- Problem
- Solution(s)
- Evaluation/comment.

This is a very common way of organising ideas in academic writing. It can be used for:

- a paragraph
- a section of a longer document
- a complete article
- a complete book.

Here is an example of this pattern in a short paragraph.

I am a foreign student living in Britain. I find it very difficult to meet British students. I will join some university clubs so as to meet some students. This should help to put me in contact with British students.

This pattern of organisation is presented in Reading Unit 4.

1.5 Read Text 4.1, which is an article about protecting the ozone layer and how developing countries can participate in solutions to global warming. It uses the **Situation→Problem→Solution→Evaluation** pattern of organisation.

Text 4.1

Protecting the ozone layer

Over the past year, scientific evidence has continued to mount showing that stratospheric ozone layer depletion is even more serious than thought only a few years back. This poses a major problem, because the ozone layer shields life from a harmful solar ultraviolet radiation known as UV-B. Although ozone depletion has been most pronouced at the poles, its effects will be serious at other latitudes, since UV-B, like all solar radiation, increases in intensity toward the equator. At higher latitudes, people will face a greater risk of skin cancer; at lower latitudes, more crop damage and health effects such as cataracts and immune system impairment are likely to occur; and vital links in food chains on land and sea might be broken.

While the ozone problem has been caused principally by industrialized countries, developing countries will have to join them in reaching a solution. Their participation is currently facilitated by the 1987 Montreal Protocol (MP), but if the phaseout needs to be accelerated, additional financial incentives and a more flexible way of carrying out the accord would be required.

Adapted from 'Protecting the ozone layer' by Mohan Munasinghe and Kenneth Sing, *Finance and Development*, June 1992

1.6 Complete the flow diagram below on the basis of Text 4.1:

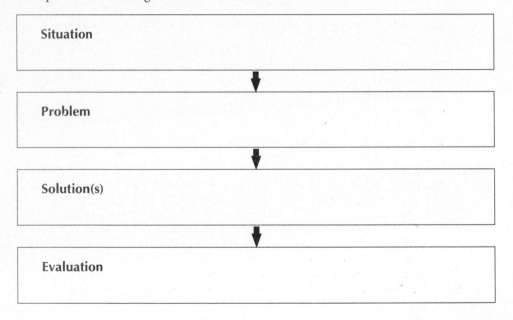

Situation

↓

Problem

↓

Solution(s)

↓

Evaluation

1.7 Compare your answers with those of a partner.

1.8 Is there a further problem created by the proposed solution in the text?

 Step 3

Text 4.2 is about the harmful substances emitted by paints. The sentences have been arranged in the wrong order.

1.9 Decide how to arrange the sentences in a more logical order, as they would probably have been arranged in the original article. Keep in mind the **Situation→ Problem→Solution→Evaluation** pattern. Make notes on the reasons for your choices.

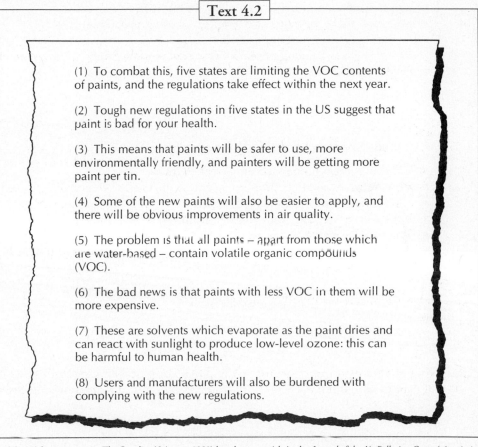

Text 4.2

(1) To combat this, five states are limiting the VOC contents of paints, and the regulations take effect within the next year.

(2) Tough new regulations in five states in the US suggest that paint is bad for your health.

(3) This means that paints will be safer to use, more environmentally friendly, and painters will be getting more paint per tin.

(4) Some of the new paints will also be easier to apply, and there will be obvious improvements in air quality.

(5) The problem is that all paints – apart from those which are water-based – contain volatile organic compounds (VOC).

(6) The bad news is that paints with less VOC in them will be more expensive.

(7) These are solvents which evaporate as the paint dries and can react with sunlight to produce low-level ozone: this can be harmful to human health.

(8) Users and manufacturers will also be burdened with complying with the new regulations.

Adapted from a report in *The Guardian* (6 August 1989) based on an article in the *Journal of the Air Pollution Control Association* (vol 39:517)

1.10 Decide how your new order of sentences can be grouped into paragraphs.

1.11 Compare your answers with those of a partner. Be prepared to give specific reasons for your choices.

TASK 2

In this task you will write an article on the following topic:

Reducing global warming: what each individual can do

The article is to appear in a student magazine and will be read by people like yourself. It should be about 500 words in length. The purpose is to:

- inform readers of the problem
- suggest some possible solutions
- suggest how each individual can help in his or her daily life
- show how these solutions also give rise to other problems.

If you are using the Reading book in this series, you may want to review the texts in Unit 4 on global warming.

 Step 1

2.1 Ask yourself the following pre-writing questions:

- What do I already know about global warming?
- Who are my readers? Is the student magazine local or national?
- What do my readers already know about the subject?
- What will my readers want to learn from me about the subject?
- What will probably be my readers' attitude towards global warming?
- How can I make my article interesting, especially to readers who have little interest in the subject?

2.2 Discuss these questions with a partner.

 Step 2

2.3 Using the brainstorming method, write down your ideas in note form as quickly as you can, in any order. As before, try to achieve a rapid and spontaneous 'flow' of ideas.

2.4 Now plan your article by thinking about the order and grouping of your ideas.

- Try to arrange your ideas in a logical order.
- Decide how your points can be grouped together, so that each group has one main or unifying idea.
- Decide how your groups of points can be arranged effectively in a **Situation→Problem→Solution→Evaluation** pattern.
- Add notes about further information or ideas, if necessary, to support your main ideas.

2.5 Find a partner and exchange plans. When you read your partner's plan, ask yourself:

- Is the order of points effective?
- Will each group of points form a well-organised paragraph?

- Is the order of groups of points – i.e. paragraphs – effective?
- Do the paragraphs form an effective **Situation→Problem→Solution→Evaluation** pattern of organisation?

Try to identify both strengths and weaknesses in the plan. Discuss your ideas with your partner. Use the evaluation checklists (in Units 2 and 3) and Appendices 1 and 2 to guide you.

2.6 Think critically about your partner's comments. Which comments do you agree with? Why? Which comments do you disagree with? Why? Try to improve your plan.

 Step 3

2.7 Write your first draft.

2.8 When you have finished writing your first draft, re-read it. Then ask yourself the following post-writing questions:

- Is there a clear definition of global warming?
- What specific evidence have I given?
- Is this evidence relevant?
- What solutions have I given? Are they practical?
- Do these solutions concentrate on what *each individual* can do in his or her daily life?
- Is there too much emphasis on what organisations and governments – rather than individuals – can do?
- Does the essay begin and end in an interesting way?
- Is the **Situation→Problem→Solution→Evaluation** sequence effectively carried through in the essay as a whole?

 Step 4

2.9 Exchange drafts with a partner.

2.10 Apply the post-writing questions in 2.8 to your partner's draft.

2.11 Refer to Evaluation Checklist A or B for further questions to consider when reading your partner's draft. If you use Evaluation Checklist A, concentrate on Sections 2 and 4. If you use Evaluation Checklist B, concentrate on Sections 2 and 3.

2.12 Make written comments and suggestions for improvement on your partner's draft or on another piece of paper. Refer specifically to many of the post-writing questions and to the points in the relevant sections of Evaluation Checklist A or B. Add your name or initials to these comments when you make them.

2.13 Discuss your comments and suggestions with your partner. Think critically about your partner's comments. Which comments do you agree with? Why? Which comments do you disagree with? Why? Try to be specific in answering these questions.

 ## Step 5

2.14 Refer either to Sections 5 and 6 of Evaluation Checklist A or to Sections 4 and 6 of Evaluation Checklist B, and to Appendices 1 and 2, to help you make further improvements to your own draft.

2.15 Rewrite your draft, with corrections and improvements, and give it to your teacher.

TASK 3 (OPTIONAL)

WRITING CONFERENCE

The writing conference is an opportunity for you to assess the progress in your academic writing in English by taking an overall view of a number of essays.

You can begin by evaluating some of the essays you have written in English with the aid of Evaluation Checklist B. Choose between three and five essays you have written recently.

 ## Step 1

3.1 Read the essays once.

3.2 Read Evaluation Checklist B again and make sure that all the terms are clear to you. Keep in mind the six main aspects of writing evaluation:

1. Content
2. Organisation
3. Cohesion
4. Vocabulary
5. Grammar
6. Mechanical accuracy.

 ## Step 2

3.3 Take a sheet of paper and divide it into two columns. Write 'Strengths' as the heading on the left and 'Weaknesses' as the heading on the right.

3.4 Re-read your essays and make notes in each of the columns as you read. With the aid of Evaluation Checklist B, look for strengths and weaknesses that occur *in more than one essay* – often enough to form a pattern. Ask yourself, for example:

- Is the content in my essays consistently relevant and well-developed?
- Do I have consistent problems with organisation?
- Do I make repeated mistakes with the use of the present perfect tense?

These are only a few examples of the kinds of questions you can ask yourself in the process of trying to evaluate your writing. Try not to rely wholly on the teacher's comments about your essay – leave some room for your own independent analysis.

3.5 Be *specific* in what you write; for example, if you feel that you have frequent problems with grammar, identify which problems they are. For instance, are they associated with:

- the present perfect tense?
- definite or indefinite articles?
- agreement of subject and verb?

The more specific you are in your assessment, the more you will learn from it. To help you, use a good learner's grammar such as *Using English Grammar: Meaning and Form* (Woods and MacLeod, Prentice Hall International, 1990) or *Collins Cobuild English Grammar* (Collins Cobuild, 1991.)

 Step 3

3.6 Once you have completed this process and made notes in both columns, make some further notes about your conclusions. Try to comment on questions like these:

- Do I feel my writing is improving? Why/why not?
- Which weaknesses or mistakes occur most often in my writing? Which ones are the most serious?
- In what areas do I need to concentrate most for improvement? Why?
- What are the most obvious strengths in my writing?
- How can I build on these strengths in future essays?
- What can I say about my writing as a whole?

You can probably think of other questions to ask yourself about your writing. Remember that the aim is to achieve a *balanced* view. It is often easier to identify weaknesses than strengths in your writing and to be too negative in your assessment. Both strengths and weaknesses should be clear in your mind, and you can discuss these with your teacher. Take your essays and written evaluation with you when you meet your teacher.

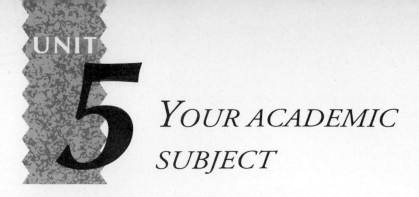

UNIT 5

YOUR ACADEMIC SUBJECT

TASK 1

In Unit 4, you wrote a definition of global warming as part of your essay. In Unit 3 you did some work on categorising and may have used a classification diagram to help you organise your information. Both of these language functions will be put to use in this unit.

The topic is:

Define and justify your subject or profession

If you are using the Reading book in this series, you will have worked on formal definition and extended definition in Units 4 and 5.

 Step 1

1.1 Study the following definition. Is there any extra information that you might need in order to make clear sense of the definition for a non-specialist?

Psycholinguistics: A branch of linguistics which studies the correlation between linguistic behaviour and the psychological processes thought to underlie that behaviour.

From Crystal, D. (ed.) 1980, *A First Dictionary of Linguistics and Phonetics*, Longman, London

1.2 Make notes about the definition given in 1.1 and discuss them with other students. Do you agree?

Before you go on to 1.3 and 1.4 below, you may want to make a classification diagram to help you organise the essential information about your subject into groups or categories. (See Unit 3, 2.3.)

1.3 Write a definition of your own subject or profession for other members of your group, using only one sentence.

1.4 Expand your definition into a short paragraph of extended definition which would make it clear to a non-specialist.

1.5 Exchange your extended definition with at least one other person in your group. Ask each other the following questions and discuss your answers in relation to your definitions:

- What information should a definition written for non-specialists contain?
- How should the information be organised?
- How can the information be expressed?
- Is the definition clear and helpful for the non-specialist? Why/why not?

 Step 2

1.6 What do you think we mean by the term *justifying* in an academic context? Write a concise definition of what you think it means to justify a subject or point of view.

1.7 Compare your definition with those of others in your group.

Step 3

1.8 Read the points on the question sheet on page 44. Discuss them with a partner.

1.9 Your teacher will suggest discussion of these points in relation to a specific subject or subjects.

In Task 2 you will write an essay defining and justifying your own subject or profession. In preparation for this, think again about how you can apply the points on the question sheet to your own subject or profession.

TASK 2

Here you are going to write an essay which makes an extended definition and justification of your subject or profession for non-specialist readers. The essay should be between 500 and 600 words in length.

Before you begin, think about the following points:

- Who are the non-specialist readers you are writing for?
- In what form do you want your essay to be published or presented?

 Step 1

2.1 Before writing your first draft, think again about how you can apply the points on the question sheet on page 44 to your own subject or profession.

2.2 Ask yourself the following pre-writing questions:

- What are my readers likely to know about my subject or profession?
- What will my readers want to learn from me about the subject?
- What will probably be my readers' attitude towards my subject?
- How can I make my essay
  - clear
  - persuasive
  - interesting

  especially for readers who have little interest in the subject?

2.3 Discuss these questions with a partner.

 Step 2

2.4 Take the extended definition of your subject which you wrote in Task 1. Formulate an essay plan which will develop this definition more fully *and* justify your subject. If you made a classification diagram of the different aspects of your subject in 1.2, this can be used as the basis of your plan.

2.5 Think about the order and grouping of your ideas.

- Try to arrange your ideas in a logical order.
- Decide how your points can be grouped together, so that each group has one main or unifying idea when it becomes a paragraph.
- Add notes about further information or ideas which might be necessary to support your main ideas.
- Remove ideas which are not relevant to non-specialist readers.

2.6 Find a partner and exchange plans. When you read your partner's plan, ask yourself:

- Is the order of points effective?
- Will each group of points form a well-organised paragraph?

- Is the order of groups of points – i.e. paragraphs – effective?
- Is each main idea supported and developed with enough specific examples or evidence?

Try to identify both strengths and weaknesses in the plan. Discuss your ideas with your partner.

2.7 Think critically about your partner's comments. Which comments do you agree with? Why? Which comments do you disagree with? Why? Try to improve your plan.

 Step 3

2.8 Write your first draft. Indicate clearly on your draft the choices you have made about:

- your specific audience of non-specialist readers
- the form in which you would want the essay to be published or presented.

2.9 When you have finished writing your draft, re-read it. Ask yourself the following post-writing question:

Is the content of my essay appropriate for both the audience and context I have chosen?

2.10 Refer to Evaluation Checklist A (Unit 2) or Evaluation Checklist B (Unit 3) for further points to apply to your draft. If you use Evaluation Checklist A, concentrate on Sections 2, 3 and 4. If you use Evaluation Checklist B, concentrate on Sections, 1, 2 and 3.

 Step 4

2.11 Exchange drafts with a partner.

2.12 Apply the post-writing question in 2.9 to your partner's draft.

2.13 Apply to your partner's draft the points from Evaluation Checklist A or B which you used in 2.10.

2.14 Make written comments for suggestion or improvement on the draft or on another piece of paper. Refer specifically to the post-writing question and to the points in the relevant sections of Evaluation Checklist A or B. Add your name or initials to these comments when you make them.

2.15 Discuss your comments and suggestions with your partner. Think critically about your partner's comments. Which comments do you agree with? Why? Which comments do you disagree with? Why? Try to be specific in answering these questions.

Step 5

2.16 Refer either to Sections 5 and 6 of Evaluation Checklist A or to Sections 4 and 6 of Evaluation Checklist B to help you make further improvements to your own draft.

2.17 Rewrite your draft, with corrections and improvements, and give it to your teacher.

Question sheet

1. What counts as accepted knowledge and expertise in your field? Are some ideas or practices excluded because they are considered to be unorthodox or dangerous? If so, why?

2. Do people who don't belong to your field have any opportunity to challenge the assumptions and applications of your subject?

   Assumptions are things which are taken as facts or believed to be true without proof. For instance, some people assume that people of a different race, class or culture from themselves are inferior in intelligence and ability.

   Applications are the practical uses of ideas, techniques and products. For instance, one of the applications of fibre optics has been the development of medical equipment for the internal examination of the human digestive tract.

3. Whose interests are actually served by your subject? Are they the interests of, for instance, a closed community of scholars, a closed group of practitioners, an industrial sector, the ordinary citizen?

   Interests are connections from which one can make a financial profit or other form of gain, such as promotion, career advancement or political advantage. For instance,

the agrochemical industry has an interest in discouraging the growth of organic farming, which does not use chemicals for pest control, because the industry derives its profits from the sale of agro-chemicals. In other words, the agrochemical industry's interests are not best served by a widespread move to organic farming.

4. What is the relationship between your subject and vested interests in either your own country or the world outside?

   Vested interests are shares or rights in something which are of advantage to a person or organisation, and which they are usually unwilling to lose, even for the good of others. For instance, the automobile industry has a vested interest in making sure that the market for motor vehicles increases, even though motor vehicles make a major contribution to atmospheric pollution and global warming.

5. What is the connection between your subject and the life of the ordinary citizen? Is this relationship a beneficial one for the ordinary citizen?

6. How does knowledge in your subject affect (a) your own community and (b) the world beyond your community?

Definitions based on *The Longman Dictionary of Contemporary English* 1987, Longman, London

UNIT 6
INTERNATIONAL TOURISM

This unit will give you practice in:

1. Summarising information from sources.

2. Writing extended definitions.

3. Selecting relevant information from sources.

4. Combining information from several sources.

5. Developing an argument.

6. Writing a complete paper which defines a topic, presents a problem and argues for a solution.

7. Evaluating the organisation of your own and another person's essay.

8. Evaluating your draft and another person's draft with the aid of a checklist.

9. Rewriting and improving your draft.

If you are using the Reading book in this series you will have analysed texts about the changing nature of international diplomacy in Unit 6. The texts in this unit focus on a related subject: the changes taking place on an international scale in tourism.

TASK 1

 Step 1

1.1 Discuss the following questions:

- What is a tourist? How does a tourist differ from a traveller or a temporary resident?

- Have you ever been a tourist? (If you are studying outside your own country, you will be a tourist from time to time.)

- How do you feel about tourism?

- What arguments can be made for and against tourism in your country?

1.2 Write a formal definition of tourism, using only one sentence. It will be helpful to refer back to the work you did on writing definitions in Unit 5.

 Step 2

1.3 Extend your definition by discussing three or more of the following questions:

1. What are the essential functions of tourism?
2. What are the component parts or activities of tourism?
3. What different types of tourism are there?
4. How does tourism compare with other activities like travelling, shopping, entertainment, sport?
5. What other activities are connected with tourism? Are all of these activities desirable or morally acceptable?
6. Where and when did tourism originate?
7. What effects does tourism have on people and places?
8. What is the value of tourism for (a) the tourist and (b) the country in which it takes place?

TASK 2

In this task, you will be summarising and analysing a number of related texts on the topic of tourism. This will prepare you for Task 3, in which you will write your own essay on an aspect of this topic.

Text 6.1

2.1 What problem has the writer identified? Summarise Text 6.1, using no more than two sentences.

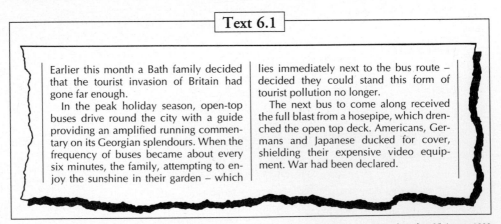

Text 6.1

Earlier this month a Bath family decided that the tourist invasion of Britain had gone far enough.

In the peak holiday season, open-top buses drive round the city with a guide providing an amplified running commentary on its Georgian splendours. When the frequency of buses became about every six minutes, the family, attempting to enjoy the sunshine in their garden – which lies immediately next to the bus route – decided they could stand this form of tourist pollution no longer.

The next bus to come along received the full blast from a hosepipe, which drenched the open top deck. Americans, Germans and Japanese ducked for cover, shielding their expensive video equipment. War had been declared.

Adapted from 'Wish you weren't here' by Frank Barrett, *The Independent*, 15 August 1990

Text 6.2

2.2 Text 6.2 is adapted from the same article as Text 6.1. What point is the writer trying to make clear to the reader in Text 6.2?

Text 6.2

Nobody objected to foreign tourists when they were a civilised trickle of intelligent aesthetes keen to explore our cathedrals, inspect our museums, absorb our culture. In the last couple of years, the trickle appears to have become an uncontrolled flood.

In the first five months of the year, the number of overseas visitors coming to Britain increased by 6 per cent to 6.3 million. In the past 12 months, Britain has received 17.5 million visitors. Between 1983 and 1988 the number of nights spent by overseas visitors in Oxford increased by 44 per cent, in York by 33 per cent, in Bath by 38 per cent and in Canterbury by 33 per cent.

The streets of these 'honeypot' cities and, of course, London, have become summer battlegrounds. Tourists arrive in vast armies, fortified with burgers, ice-creams and cans of fizzy drinks, anxious to acquire a takeaway piece of British Heritage.

The Government apparently studies these developments with a telescope placed to its blind eye. While other European countries, such as France, Spain and Italy, attempt to plan their tourism industry with the sort of seriousness appropriate to the major economic activity it has become (tourism will be the world's biggest industry within the next 10 years), the British Government avoids any sort of approach that smacks of centralised planning.

Adapted from 'Wish you weren't here' by Frank Barrett, *The Independent*, 15 August 1990

2.3 Summarise Text 6.2, using no more than three sentences.

2.4 Discuss the writer's attitude towards tourism in Texts 6.1 and 6.2.

Text 6.3

2.5 Each paragraph in Text 6.3 deals with one topic. What is the topic of each paragraph?

Text 6.3

The Romans had their villas in the Bay of Naples, the Middle Ages their crusades and pilgrimages. But consider these statistics. One hundred thousand people went on the First Crusade, an early version of the package tour, in 1096. Before 1939 an estimated million travelled abroad each year. Now, after three decades of frantic growth, there are more than 400 million a year, plus another billion-and-a-half domestic travellers. By 2000, there could be up to 650 million international trippers, and four or five times as many travelling in their own countries: 3 billion or more in transit. These are mass movements without parallel in history.

What underpins them is an immense – and still unsatisfied – appetite for travel. Tourism has so far remained a phenomenon largely of the developed world: 70 per cent of it comes from only 20 of the world's 233 states. What of the rest? Only 7 million Japanese went abroad last year: another 30–50 million may be on the way. Surveys indicate that the East European desire for travel is overwhelming. Many Pacific Rim countries – Taiwan, South Korea, Hong Kong – are getting rich.

So astonishing are the forecasts that many analysts cannot credit them. To take just one example: the Mediterranean coast-line's resident population of 130 million swells by 100 million tourists each year; United Nations projections say visitors could number 760 million by 2025. Christopher Tugendhat, chairman of the Civil Aviation Authority, has hinted at the prospect of air traffic being 'capped'. Others talk of lack of hotels or aircraft, of fuel rationing and priority permits. The only certainties, for the traveller, are delays and congestion.

Adapted from 'Death by tourism' by David Nicholson-Lord, *The Independent on Sunday*, 5 August 1990

2.6 Summarise Text 6.3 using no more than three sentences.

Text 6.4

2.7, 2.8 Identify the main idea in each paragraph in Text 6.4. What is the function of the second paragraph in relation to the first? In other words, what or how does it add to the first paragraph?

Text 6.4

The economic advantages of tourism have been greatly exaggerated. Although many third world countries sell holidays, their people are often too poor to travel. Tourist complexes in the poorer countries are outposts of Western capitalism. They are, in many cases, foreign-owned and built from imported materials to supply alien needs. Tourism draws people off the land (sometimes forcibly) so that food, too, has to be imported. Tax breaks for hotel chains and developers mean, absurdly, that the world's poorest people are subsidising the holidays of its richest. In the process, a new 'one-crop' economy is born, vulnerable to the whims of Western consumer fashion and the financial dictates of the tour operators.

A large number of examples over the last two decades illustrate such processes. Instead of the benefits of tourism 'trickling down' to the local people, they are, according to Chayant Pholpoke, founder of an anti-tourist group in Thailand, 'trickling up and out of the country'. In Tahiti, even the dancing girls' sarongs are imported. Two hundred people, an entire village, perform the famous Kecak dance in Bali: one study showed that the village was paid $20 (£11) – 10 cents a performer – while tourists paid £250 in entrance fees to the operators. In the Pacific, three-quarters of revenues go to the multinational tour companies. Nevertheless, tour companies tell holiday-makers to go out and haggle for bargains.

Adapted from 'Death by tourism' by David Nicholson-Lord, *The Independent on Sunday*, 5 August 1990

2.9 Summarise Text 6.4, using no more than two sentences. How much information from the second paragraph do you need to include?

Texts 6.5 and 6.6

2.10 In Unit 4 you focused on the **Situation**→**Problem**→**Solution**→**Evaluation** pattern of organisation commonly used in academic writing to identify and discuss a problem. Read and discuss Texts 6.5 and 6.6. Which parts of these texts deal with:

- situation?
- problem?
- solution?
- evaluation?

Text 6.5

At the conclusion of a two-day televised symposium on tourism in Osaka last October, all four visiting speakers were asked to give their final message to the Japanese. Sir Edmund Hillary, the conqueror of Everest, who should know about damage to mountains, suddenly electrified the audience by cutting though the empty discussion about international responsibility that should go with economic success and saying: 'Don't go around the world clustered together in great bus-loads. Go in twos and threes or fours and you will enjoy it much more and find yourselves much more welcome.'

Adapted from 'Pros and cons of tourism' by Roy Jenkins, *The Independent Magazine*, 7 April 1990

Text 6.6

Green tourism was born in France and articulated in Switzerland. A green holiday, typically, is nature-orientated, active, educational, tucked away harmoniously in the countryside, avoiding the crowds, relying on the welcome of local people. Green holidays mean French gites, English farmhouses. They mean bird-watching, cycling, nature-trekking, learning about foreign landscapes and cultures. They mean going back to the same place repeatedly and, often, staying with local in their homes.

Green tourism faces a paradox, though. If it insists on smallness of scale, it risks justifying the criticisms that it is merely a small market for the well-intentioned middle class. If it aims at the masses, it may be an even greater threat to landscapes and cultures.

One answer is to isolate the tourists in purpose-built, culturally sterilised holiday ghettos. Such destinations as Bali and the Maldives quarantine tourism on designated beaches and islands: in the Maldives, tourists are banned from even swimming near inhabited islands. Sterilising tourism in reservations stops the host culture being infected. Yet they are only a partial and temporary solution.

Adapted from 'Death by tourism' by David Nicholson-Lord, *The Independent on Sunday*, 5 August 1990

TASK 3

You have now covered the following:

- definition of tourism
- statements of problems
- suggested solutions.

The next step is to write an essay on the following topic:

Tourism: what can be done?

Your essays should define the topic, present the problem(s) and argue for a solution or solutions. Try to relate the problems associated with tourism to your own experience or to the situation in your own country. You can select relevant information and ideas from Texts 6.1–6.6 and from Text 6.7 on pages 53–55. The essay can be about 500 to 600 words in length.

Discuss and take notes on the following questions:

- Who are the specific audience or readers you want to write for?
- In what form do you want your essay to be published or presented?

 Step 1

3.1 Before planning your essay, make notes from Texts 6.1–6.6 and Text 6.7. Select relevant information and ideas from these texts.

3.2 Ask yourself the following pre-writing questions:

- What do I already know about tourism?
- What do my readers already know about the subject?
- What will my readers want to learn from me about the subject?
- What will probably be my readers' attitude towards tourism?
- How can I make my article interesting, especially to readers who have little interest in the subject?

Refer to your notes and discuss these questions with a partner, whose answers may be different from your own.

 Step 2

3.3 Write down your ideas in note form as quickly as you can, in any order, using the brainstorming method. As in previous writing tasks, try to achieve a rapid and spontaneous 'flow' of ideas.

3.4 Now plan your essay by thinking about the order and grouping of your ideas:

- Try to arrange your ideas in a more logical order.
- Decide how your points can be grouped together, so that each group has one main or unifying idea.
- Decide how your groups of points can be arranged effectively in a **Situation→ Problem→Solution→Evaluation** pattern.
- Add notes about further information or ideas which might be necessary to support your main ideas.

You can use the following outline as a guide to organising your ideas if you wish:

Organisation of essay	
Definition:	What is tourism?
Situation:	What is the present situation regarding tourism? How did it come about? What are the main features of the situation?
Problem:	Is there a problem? If so, what is it?
Solution/ Response:	How can the problem be dealt with? What alternative solutions are there? What constraints are there on each possible solution?
Evaluation:	Which of the solutions is likely to be the most effective? What would be the result of applying each of the solutions?

3.5 Find a partner and exchange essay plans. When you read your partner's plan, ask yourself:

- Is the order of points effective?
- Will each group of points form a well-organised paragraph?
- Is the order of groups of points – i.e. paragraphs – effective?
- Do the paragraphs from an effective **Situation→Problem→Solution→ Evaluation** pattern of organisation?

Try to identify both strengths and weaknesses in the plan. Discuss your ideas with your partner.

3.6 Think critically about your partner's comments. Which comments do you agree with? Why? Which comments do you disagree with? Why? Try to improve your plan.

Step 3

3.7 Write your first draft. Indicate clearly on your draft the choices you have made about:

- the audience or readers for whom you are writing
- the form in which you would want the essay published or presented.

3.8 When you have finished writing your draft, re-read it. Then ask yourself the following post-writing questions:

- Is there a clear definition of tourism?
- What specific evidence does the writer give to support the main ideas?
- Is this evidence relevant?
- What solutions does the writer give? Are they practical?
- Does the writer begin and end in an interesting way?
- Is there a logical problem-solving sequence?

 Step 4

3.9 Exchange drafts with a partner.

3.10 Apply the post-writing questions in 3.8 to your partner's draft.

3.11 Refer to Evaluation Checklist A (page 21) or Evaluation Checklist B (page 29) for further questions to apply to your partner's draft. If you use Evaluation Checklist A, concentrate on Sections 2 and 4. If you use Evaluation Checklist B, concentrate on Sections 2 and 3.

3.12 Make written comments and suggestions for improvement on your partner's draft or on another piece of paper. Refer specifically to many of the post-writing questions and to the points in the relevant sections of Evaluation Checklist A or B. Add your name or initials to these comments when you make them.

3.13 Discuss your comments and suggestions with your partner. Think critically about your partner's comments. Which comments do you agree with? Why? Which comments do you disagree with? Why? Try to be specific in answering these questions.

 Step 5

3.14 To help you make further improvements to your own draft, refer to the appendices and either to Sections 5 and 6 of Evaluation Checklist A or to Sections 4 and 6 of Evaluation Checklist B.

3.15 Rewrite your draft, with corrections and improvements, and give it to your teacher.

Discussion

How do the texts on tourism in this unit relate to the texts you have read in Reading Unit 6 on international diplomacy?

Text 6.7

TOURISM'S GLOBAL IMPACT

Deforestation

The loss of forest cover from tourist facilities and heavy traffic: causes include holiday developments, pollution.

Nepal: Wood for trekkers, furniture for accommodation.

Dominican Republic: More than a million trees cut down for golf courses.

Alps: forests cut down for skiing facilities and 40,000 km of ski runs. Damage from four-wheel drives, off-piste skiing. Deforestation causes floods and mudslides.

Water pollution

Water and sea pollution and dirty beaches, resulting from the disposal of untreated sewage, litter and other waste.

Mediterranean: Estimated one-third of all tourism takes place around shores: tourism a principal cause of pollution. Dirtiest sea in the world: 85 per cent of waste water near coast goes directly into sea. Sewage contamination widespread, causing outbreaks of cholera, typhoid, hepatitis and dysentery. Low tidal range makes beaches vulnerable. Needs 80 years to renew its waters.

German coast: Salmonella outbreaks from toilets in cruising boats.

Pyrenees: Sewage discharge into streams.

Caribbean: Second most popular holiday destination, after Mediterranean: 170 million residents, 100 million tourists. 90 per cent of waste dumped untreated into sea. Pollution destroying mangrove forests, seagrass beds, coral reefs.

Ecosystems

Threatened landscapes, ecosystems and habitats, on land and sea: uplands, reefs and mangrove forests.

Carribbean: Yacht anchors damage coral reefs.

Venezuela: Tourist agencies use dioxin to kill seaweed. Several million fish killed.

Teide National Park, Canary Islands: Alien seeds carried by visitors disrupt native flora.

Kashmir: Heli-skiing, banned in parts of West, threatens mountain ecology.

Africa, Mounts Kenya and Kilimanjaro, Amboseli and Ngorongoro National Parks: Foot safaris, off-road and night driving. Landscape erosion, wild-life disruption.

Caribbean: Coral reef loss – up to 80 per cent in Anguilla.

Coto Donana and Ebro Delta: Spolec Wetlands threatened by planned tourist and leisure complexes.

Camargue, France: Tourism complexes threaten wetlands.

Po Delta, Italy: Holiday developments.

Oristano Wetlands, Sardinia: Holiday developments.

Great Barrier Reef, Queensland, Australia: Coastal mangroves destroyed for tourist facilities, threatening reef with sediment.

East African coast, including Mauritius, Reunion, the Seychelles, Kenya and Tanzania: Damage to coral reefs from trophy-hunting. One expert says there may be more coral from Mauritius and Reunion on the West's coffee tables than remains in their own waters.

Wildlife trade

Trade in wildlife trophies and souvenirs: threat to coral reefs, species and habitats. Much of this trade is illegal.

Seychelles: Airport shops sell turtle products.

Kenya: Shops sell shells, coral.

Caribbean: Turtle souvenirs sold.

Greece: Illegal fur sales widespread: lynx, ocelot, leopard, cheetah, panther and jaguar.

Bali: Turtles, including seriously endangered hawksbill, killed for tourist souvenirs and restaurant food.

Philippines: Coral, giant clam and queen conch souvenirs on sale.

Africa: Shells, corals, horns, trophies, crocodile skins, rare plants sold for souvenirs.

Far East including Hong Kong: Extensive trade in wildlife souvenirs, including ivory, elephant skins.

Threatened species

Endangered species at risk from loss of habitat to tourism, pollution and the illegal trade in trophies, souvenirs.

East African national parks: Harassment of big mammals by safari vehicles.

Spain, Canary Islands: Chimpanzees, lions and tiger cubs used by beach photographers. Animals drugged and killed young. Estimated 10 chimps die in the wild for every cub caught.

Greece, Turkey: Most loggerhead turtle breeding sites on beaches destroyed.

Mediterranean: Dolphin numbers reduced, monk seal endangered by pollution and loss of habitat.

Caribbean: Species threatened, some possibly extinct, include monk seal, manatee, alligators and crocodiles, dolphins, turtles. Tourism a major contributory cause, through pollution, habitat loss, souvenir trade.

Air pollution

Air pollution, smog, fumes, including acid rain and discharges from car exhausts, caused by high tourist traffic.

Chiang Mai, Northern Thailand: Sacred mountain and monastery often invisible in smog from traffic.

Alps: Traffic causes pollution; 60 per cent of forests damaged by acid rain.

Queues

Visitor 'honeypots': the most visited destinations where pressure of numbers has led to congestion and damage.

Nepal: Litter and human waste from trekkers.

Kakadu National Park, Northern Territory, Australia: visitor numbers quadrupled since film Crocodile Dundee.

Inca Trail, Machupicchu, Peru: Trekkers damaging Inca remains, making campfires in ruins, leaving garbage.

Venice: City closed in 1987 because of crowds. Sculptures worn away.

Leaning Tower, Pisa: Restricted access.

Parthenon, Athens: Restricted access.

York, UK: Residents sport anti-tourist badges.

Tower of London, Canterbury Cathedral: Stonework wearing away.

Pyramids, Egypt: Stonework damaged.

Lascaux, Dordogne: Cave of prehistoric paintings closed, replica built.

Notre Dame, Paris: 10.8 million visitors yearly. Coach emissions damage stonework.

Sistine Chapel, Rome: Humidity from visitors harming frescoes.

Clovelly, Devon: Visitors pay to enter village.

Lake District, Peak District, UK: Footpath erosion, stone wall damage, traffic jams.

United States national parks: Closures, e.g. Yosemite, Mount Rushmore.

Stonehenge, UK: Restricted access.

Resources

Strains on local resources including water, electricity and food: higher demand by tourist facilities for supplies.

Kenya: Coastal fishing villages displaced for tourism.

Portugal: Loss of farmland to hotels, golf courses.

Caribbean: Over-fishing of seafood, e.g. lobster and conch. Electricity and water shortages, e.g. Granada, Antigua.

Ko Samui, Thailand: Disposal facilities for only 25 per cent of tourist waste. Water shortages.

Tunisia: Farm irrigation affected by hotels.

Goa: Hotels get piped water, villages without it.

Beach erosion

Beach erosion, loss of dunes, caused by excavation for sand to be used in construction of hotels and airports.

Negros, Philippines: Sand taken for tourist airport – massive beach losses.

West Africa: Beaches 'mined' for hotels.

Caribbean: Sand taken for hotels, Grenada and Antigua. Beach erosion, danger to sea defences.

Goa: Sand dunes destroyed.

Urbanisation

Tourist developments, holiday resorts and accommodation, leisure complexes, urban sprawl, infrastructures.

Mediterranean, particularly Spain, France, Italy, Greece: Tourist-related development. Up to 760 million visitors each year by 2025, more than seven times present total – 95 per cent of coast could be urbanised. Wetlands, forests, Maquis shrublands already devastated. Turkish coast the latest to be threatened.

Nepal: Hotel and lodge building.

Hawaii: Over-development into 'concrete jungle', e.g. Waikiki.

Ladakh: Tourist facilities leading to urban sprawl.

Alps: Ski complexes, holiday homes (up to 50 per cent in places), 15,000 ski lifts and cable cars. Ski-lift use growing at 5 per cent a year. Mountain villages transformed into suburbs.

Antarctica: Plans by Chile, Australia for development.

UK Lake District and other national parks: Holiday complexes, second homes – 40 per cent of houses empty in some parishes.

Goa: Hotels breaking planning rules.

The Independent on Sunday, 5 August 1990

UNIT 7

INTERNATIONAL STUDENTS

This unit will give you practice in:

1. Interpreting statistical data presented in tabulated form.

2. Incorporating such data in an essay.

3. Distinguishing between personal and impersonal styles of argument.

4. Showing differences in accountability for ideas in a discussion or argument.

5. Writing an essay presenting an argument in an appropriate style.

6. Evaluating the organisation of your own and another person's essay.

TASK 1

In this part of the unit you will be working with statistics. In Task 5 you will have a chance to use some of these statistics in a writing assignment.

 Step 1

1.1 Study Tables 7.1 and 7.2. These deal with student trends in a university.

- What was the percentage of international students to UK students in (a) 1992 and (b) 1993?
- What kind of countries do most of the international students come from?
- What is likely to be the source of funding for most international students?
- What would you expect the percentage of international students to have been in 1994?

 Step 2

1.2 Read Table 7.2. What differences in financing do you find between:

(a) undergraduates and postgraduates?
(b) students from developed and developing countries?

In other words, who is likely to be paying for the international students – government agencies or private individuals?

Table 7.1

Redlands University: Total numbers and % proportions of students in November 1992 and 1993

	1992 No.	1993 No.	1992 %	1993 %
All students	7639	8247	100.0	100.0
UK students	5929	6560	77.6	78.3
International students	1710	1787	22.4	21.7
Developed countries	472	549	6.2	6.7
Commonwealth	26	23		
European Community	296	391		
Other	150	135		
Developing countries	1239	1238	16.2	15.0
Commonwealth	646	629		
European Community	154	193		
Other	439	416		

Source: Dept of Employment, EIU estimates

Table 7.2

Redlands University: Financing of full-time international students, November 1992 and 1993

	Family/Self		Sponsor		Total	
	1992	1993	1992	1993	1992	1993
Undergraduates						
Developed countries	178	195	127	154	305	349
Developing countries	348	351	123	131	471	482
Total	526	546	250	285	776	831
Postgraduates						
Developed countries	89	117	77	83	166	200
Developing countries	186	182	582	574	768	756
Total	275	299	659	657	934	956
All						
Developed countries	267	312	204	237	471	549
Developing countries	534	533	705	705	1239	1238
TOTAL	801	845	909	942	1710	1787

Source: Dept of Employment, EIU estimates

1.3 As an international student yourself, what are your views on the trends shown in Tables 7.1 and 7.2?

Task 2

Step 1

On the whole, students from developing countries come from outside the European Union and will therefore pay full-cost fees, whereas United Kingdom and European Union students pay a lower 'home' fee.

2.1 If we take the international student fee as being £5,000 per postgraduate student, what would the fee income have been for 1993 from international postgraduates from developing countries?

> Fee income = £5,000 × Developing country postgraduates

The fee income from students is not, of course, the only income which either the university or the community receives. In addition, it is estimated that expenditure on goods and services is around 17 per cent more than the expenditure on fees.

2.2 If we assume that for every £1.00 spent on fees, students spend an additional £1.17 on goods and services, such as accommodation, food, transport, clothing, entertainment, etc., what would postgraduates from developing countries, attending Redlands University, have spent on goods and services in 1993?

> Total expenditure on goods & services = £5,000 × £1.17 × No. of students

2.3 What conclusions can you reach as to the importance of income from international students to Redlands University and to the town of Redlands?

2.4 Write a paragraph describing the contribution made by international students to the income of Redlands University. Use information in Table 7.2.

Task 3

Step 1

3.1 Discuss these questions:

- Are there many international students or foreign workers in your country? If so, what attitudes do people in your country have towards foreign students or workers?

- What attitude do some British people have to foreign tourists? Refer back to the articles you read in Unit 6 about foreign tourists coming to Britain.

- In your experience, what do you think will be the attitudes of people in Britain, or in another foreign country you are familiar with, to foreign students or foreign workers?

 Step 2

3.2 Now read Text 7.1, which is written in a *personal* style.

Text 7.1

Dear Sir

Why are our universities and colleges full of foreign students? Why can't they stay at home instead of coming here and taking places away from our sons and daughters?

We hear a lot from the government about increasing the number of students in higher education. But when you look at the colleges and universities, you find them full of foreign students. I think this is wrong. We should give priority to our own students.

Not only do these foreigners take up university places. They also fill up accommodation so that it is difficult for our own students to find places to live. Also, most of these students have a lot of money so they can afford to pay high prices for somewhere to live. This means that home students can't afford accommodation.

I wonder what these students give in return for their time here? They come and study and take our ideas and then they return home and set up new factories. Because they have cheap labour, they can out-price us and before you know what has happened, our industries are ruined. The people who benefit are their fellow countrymen, not us.

I think the government is wrong to encourage foreign students to come here. They should stay in their own countries and allow us to give our own children the education that they and their country need.

Yours faithfully
[Name and address supplied]

3.3 How do you react to the ideas in the letter? Do you think the writer's viewpoint is understandable? Is it reasonable? What arguments can you make against the writer's viewpoint?

3.4 Summarise the arguments put forward by the correspondent.

TASK 4

Arguments can be written in either a *personal* or an *impersonal* style. In a personal style, writers show that they are committed to and accountable for the ideas they express. In an impersonal style, writers may hedge; that is, they avoid showing strong commitment to a particular idea, proposal or position. Writers who hedge too much lack credibility – their readers may not accept what they say as being reliable or truthful. It is important, therefore, to find a balance between personal and impersonal style, between being over-committed and not showing sufficient commitment.

In academic argument, it is common to be impersonal, even when the writer is personally involved in the argument. Impersonality is a way of putting a distance between the writer and the argument. It treats the argument as something separate from the writer. Likewise, it puts a distance between the reader and the argument.

In Unit 2, you wrote a letter of argument supporting the practice of sending students abroad to study. This was probably in a relatively personal style. If you are using the Reading book in this series, in Unit 7 you will find texts presenting arguments about development and cultural values. They use an impersonal, academic style.

 Step 1

4.1 Are both forms of argument common in your culture? Where and when would each one be used:

    (a) in writing?
    (b) in speaking?

Discuss.

 Step 2

4.2 To give you a better idea of stylistic differences between personal and impersonal writing, read the *impersonal* version of Text 7.1 in Text 7.2 below. What important differences do you find between the ways in which language is used in each version?

Text 7.2

Colleges and universities in this country appear to be full of international students. It could be argued that instead of coming here and taking places away from home students, international students should stay in their own countries.

The government has a policy of increasing the number of students in higher education. However, a survey of colleges and universities will reveal that the increase in numbers is made up of international rather than home students. Thus, it seems that instead of giving priority to increasing the number of home students, the higher education sector has given precedence to students from abroad. This would seem to be a misapplication of government policy.

In addition to taking up university places, international students compete for accommodation, making it difficult for home students to

---

find places to live. Furthermore, as most international students appear to be more affluent than home students, they can afford to pay higher prices for accommodation, thus inflating rental levels beyond the means of local students.

It could be asked what international students give in return for their time in this country. It appears that, having come here to study, they return to their home countries with new-found ideas which they then apply to their own commercial and industrial enterprises. Since they have cheap labour, they can out-price this country's products, so undermining the industrial sector. Thus, it appears that the beneficiaries of a policy of encouraging international students to study in this country are the foreigners themselves.

4.3 Choose one paragraph of Texts 7.1 and 7.2 for careful study. Working with a partner, make a detailed list of the differences between the two versions. Here is an example from paragraph 1.

Text 7.1	Text 7.2
Questions which assume the truth of the answer:	Statements using hedging and impersonal language:
Why are colleges and universities full of foreign students?	**Colleges appear to be full …** **It could be argued that …**

Make a similar table, listing the *personal* features in your chosen paragraph in the left-hand column under Text 7.1, and the *impersonal* features in the right-hand column under Text 7.2. Select specific words and phrases as examples.

4.4 There are several ways in which you can avoid showing commitment (hedge) in your writing.

Showing personal commitment	Hedging
Using *I, we* and *you*	Using non-personal nouns or noun phrases
Using active verbs	Using passive verbs
Using verbs like *think, believe*	Avoiding the use of verbs like *think, believe*
Making straight, unmodified statements or claims: *X is Y*	Making indirect statements: *X appears to be Y*
Making strong recommendations: *should*	Making 'soft' proposals: *may*
Attitudinal signals such as *certainly, undoubtedly, obviously, in my view*, etc.	Attitudinal signals such as *apparently, unexpectedly, surprisingly, no doubt*, etc.

See also Appendix 4 on page 71

Return to Texts 7.1 and 7.2 and find examples of ways in which the writers have shown personal commitment on the one hand and hedged (that is, avoided showing commitment) on the other.

In general, academic writers write in an impersonal style, carefully hedging their claims. Recently, though, academic style in some disciplines has been changing and it is becoming more common for writers to use the first person and to be more direct in the statements they make. In other words, academic writers are becoming more accountable and they show strength of belief. Note, however, that they do not overuse ways of showing personal commitment. They tend to do so only when it will have most effect on their reader, as you will see in Text 7.3.

TASK 5

When writing an argument – academic or otherwise – it is very important to end with an effective conclusion. The conclusion should end the argument convincingly, and it should refer back to:

- the evidence which the writer has presented
- the arguments that have been developed
- the main point or thesis, which is usually stated at the beginning in the first paragraph.

 Step 1

5.1 Which of the following conclusions would you choose to end Text 7.2? Give reasons for your choice.

1. *It could be concluded that international students should study in their own countries instead of taking places away from home students.*

2. *In conclusion, it would undoubtedly be wise for the next government to charge international students a much higher rate of residential tax than home students are expected to pay.*

3. *On the basis of these trends, it can be concluded that the policy of encouraging international students to study in this country should be replaced by one which discourages them from coming here, while simultaneously giving priority to home students. In this way, the policy of increasing student numbers would benefit the country in ways compatible with the government's intentions.*

4. *To conclude, it could be argued that home students should be encouraged to enrol in universities abroad.*

5. *The last thing that can be said is that if present trends continue, we can expect a decline in this country's economic competitiveness and, consequently, a reduction in the standard of living of its population.*

Step 2

5.2 What is the thesis or overall idea of Text 7.2? Is this thesis referred to in the conclusion you have chosen? Does the writer refer back to the evidence and arguments that have been presented earlier in the conclusion you have selected?

5.3 All the conclusions given in 5.1 contain examples of hedging. Make a list of examples of the ways in which the writer hedges.

5.4 Rephrase the conclusion you chose so as to show that you, the writer, are prepared to be accountable for what you say. Use the first person and verbs like *think* and *believe*. Compare your rephrasing with the original text. Which do you find most convincing?

 Step 3

5.5 Text 7.3 is a third version of the letter which mixes both personal and impersonal styles. When the writer wishes to be accountable, this is made clear. Likewise, when the writer wishes to hedge, an impersonal style is used.

Study Text 7.3 and list the ways in which the writer demonstrates accountability. Compare your rephrasing in Step 5.4 with the rephrasing in Text 7.3.

Text 7.3

Colleges and universities in this country appear to be full of foreign students. I would like to argue that instead of coming here and taking places away from home students, international students should stay in their own countries.

The government has a policy of increasing the number of students in higher education. However, a survey of colleges and universities will reveal that the increase in numbers is made up of foreign rather than home students. Thus, it seems to me that instead of giving priority to increasing the number of home students, the higher education sector has actually given precedence to students from abroad. In my view this is a misapplication of government policy.

In addition to taking up university places, international students compete for accommodation, making it difficult for home students to find places to live. Furthermore, as most international students appear to be more affluent than home students, they can afford to pay higher prices for accommodation, thus inflating rental levels beyond the means of local students.

It could be asked what international students give in return for their time in this country. I believe that, having come here to

---

63

study, they return to their home countries with new-found ideas which they then apply to their own commercial and industrial enterprises. Since they have cheap labour, they can out-price this country's products, so undermining the industrial sector. Thus, it appears that the beneficiaries of a policy of encouraging international students to study in this country are the foreigners themselves.

I wish to advocate replacing the present policy of encouraging international students to study in this country by one which discourages them from coming here, while simultaneously giving priority to home students. In this way, the policy of increasing student numbers would benefit this country in ways compatible with the government's intentions.

Task 6

For this task you will write a short paper as a contribution to a collection of papers, whose theme is as follows:

> **Higher education: the role of international students**

You have been told that the writer of the introductory paper in the collection will take a line very similar to that of the writer of Text 7.1. As a student, you need to argue against such a view by putting a strong case in favour of international students studying in a foreign country. Use any information you like from Tables 7.1 and 7.2. You will need to write in an academic and impersonal style but, as in Text 7.3, you can use hedging language when you want to avoid showing commitment, and direct language when you particularly wish to be accountable for the ideas you state.

 Step 1

6.1 Note as many arguments as you can in favour of international students studying in the UK (or another host country, such as Australia or the USA). Use rough notes rather than complete sentences.

6.2 Use as much objective data as you can. Refer to the information in the tables in this unit, and select information which is relevant.

Remember to cite your source when you use data. (Refer to Unit 6 in this book and to Unit 6 of Study Skills for Academic Writing in this series.)

Find other data if you can, and incorporate this data in your paper. (See the examples in Appendices 1, 2 and 3 for ways of referring to such data.)

Step 2

6.3 When you have assembled enough ideas, plan your paper by thinking about the order and grouping of your ideas.

- Try to arrange your ideas in a logical order.
- Decide how your points can be grouped together so that each group has one main or unifying idea.
- Decide on the best order for your groups of points, which will become paragraphs in your draft.
- Add notes about further information or ideas which might be necessary to support your main ideas.

6.4 Find a partner and exchange plans. When you read your partner's plan, ask yourself:

- Is the order of points effective?
- Will each group of points form a well-organised paragraph?
- Is the order of groups of points – i.e. paragraphs – effective?

Try to identify both strengths and weaknesses in the plan. Discuss your ideas with your partner.

6.5 Think critically about your partner's comments. Which comments do you agree with? Why? Which comments do you disagree with? Why? Try to improve your plan.

 Step 3

6.6 Write your first draft.

6.7 When you have finished writing your draft, re-read it. Then ask yourself the following post-writing questions:

- Are the ideas appropriate for an audience of a collection of academic papers?
- Is the argument personal or impersonal in style?
- Do I hedge too much? Am I appropriately cautious in my claims?
- Do I show personal commitment to my argument? And if so, how? Am I too committed so that I have lost objectivity?
- What specific evidence do I give to support the main ideas?
- Is this evidence relevant?
- Are sources for evidence or data cited correctly?
- Do I begin and end in an interesting way?

Step 4

6.8 Exchange drafts with a partner.

6.9 Apply the post-writing questions in 6.7 to your partner's draft.

6.10 Challenge your partner on hedged and unhedged statements. Why does your partner avoid responsibility by hedging? If your partner makes unhedged statements, suggestions, recommendations or conclusions, how strongly supported are they?

6.11 Refer to Evaluation Checklist A (on page 21) or Evaluation Checklist B (on page 29) for further questions to apply to your partner's draft. If you use Evaluation Checklist A, concentrate on Sections 2 and 4. If you use Evaluation Checklist B, concentrate on Sections 2 and 3.

6.12 Make written comments and suggestions for improvement on your partner's draft or on another piece of paper. Refer specifically to many of the post-writing questions and to the points in the relevant sections of Evaluation Checklist A or B. Add your name or initials to these comments when you make them to show that you are accountable for the points you have made about your partner's draft.

6.13 Discuss your comments and suggestions with your partner. Think critically about your partner's comments. Which comments do you agree with? Why? Which comments do you disagree with? Why? Try to be specific when answering these questions.

 Step 5

6.14 Refer either to Sections 5 and 6 of Evaluation Checklist A or Sections 4 and 5 of Evaluation Checklist B to help you make further improvements to your own draft.

6.15 Rewrite your draft, incorporating corrections and improvements, and give it to your teacher.

APPENDIX 1: COHESIVE MARKERS

'And' type
in fact
also
furthermore
apart from this
what is more
in addition
in the same way
not only … but also
as well as
besides

Example
for example
for instance
as follows:
that is to say
in this case

Stating the obvious
obviously
it goes without saying
clearly
naturally
of course
as one might expect
surely
after all

Generalising
in general
on the whole
as a rule
for the most part
speaking generally
in most cases
usually

'Or' type
in other words
to put it another way
to be more precise
or rather
alternatively

Contrast
on the other hand
alternatively
in contrast to

Equivalence
in other words
namely
that is to say

Concession
however
even though
however much …
nevertheless
still
yet

Cause and effect
because
because of this
thus
accordingly
hence
in order to
so that
in that case
under those circumstances
as a result
for this reason
as a consequence

'But' type
although
however
whereas
yet
nevertheless
despite
in spite of
on the contrary

Transition
now,
as far as X is concerned
with regard to
as for …
It follows that

Highlighting
in particular
especially
mainly
particularly

Referring
who
which
when
where
whose
that

Conclusion
so
finally,
to conclude

APPENDIX 2: MARKERS OF COMPARISON AND CONTRAST

Comparison within sentences

X is X and Y are X is	very quite rather	like Y similar similar to Y	in terms of with respect to with regard to	quality/size/ expense etc.

X resembles Y	in that	they are both large/expensive etc.

X is	exactly precisely just virtually almost nearly	the same as Y.

Both X and Y are large/expensive etc.
X is as large as Y.
X is no larger than Y.
X is the same size as Y.

X is costly to buy	and	it is (also) costly to maintain.

Comparison between sentences

X is expensive to buy.	Similarly, Likewise, Moreover, Furthermore, In addition,	it is expensive to maintain/operate etc.

Contrast within sentences

X is unlike Y X differs from Y X and Y differ X is different from Y X contrasts with Y	with respect to with regard to in terms of	size/expense etc.
	in that X is smaller/more expensive etc.	

X has four Zs,	whereas while but yet although	Y has three.

Y is X is	considerably a great deal (very) much rather somewhat a little slightly only just scarcely	smaller than X. larger than Y.

Contrast between sentences

X is expensive to buy.	However, Conversely, By/In contrast, On the other hand,	it is cheap to operate/maintain etc.

APPENDIX 3: WAYS OF REFERRING TO DATA IN TABLES AND DIAGRAMS

You can **refer** to data in tables and diagrams like this:

Table 1 shows the estimated number of visitors to the UK between 1982 and 1987.

Expenditure has been adjusted to take account of inflation during the period concerned, taking 1982 as a base.

You can **comment** on data like this:

As can be seen, there was an 85 per cent increase in real expenditure during this period.

You can use the following patterns:

As can be seen in	Table 1, the table, the graph, the diagram, Figure 1, the figure,

According to As is shown in	Table 1, Figure 2,

It can be seen from the	table graph diagram figures statistics	that ...

There was a (very)	slight small slow steady marked large steep sharp rapid	rise increase fluctuation decrease decline reduction fall drop

APPENDIX 4: WAYS OF SHOWING AND AVOIDING COMMITMENT

Ways of showing commitment

- Use first person pronoun as subject:
  I, we

- Use verbs with first person subject:
  advocate, believe, feel, know, mean, think, understand

- Use personalised expressions:
  it seems to me, it appears, from my point of view, in my view, in my opinion

- Use attitudinal signals such as:
  assuredly, certainly, definitely, indisputably, unarguably, undeniably, undoubtedly, unquestionably

  clearly, obviously, plainly

  fortunately, unfortunately, unhappily

  significantly

  rightly, wrongly

- Use verbs like *should, must, ought to*

Ways of 'hedging' or avoiding commitment

- Avoid using first person pronouns

- Use impersonal subjects, such as *it*

- Use passive voice so as to avoid specifying an agent or 'doer' such as:
  It can be imagined that …
  Large numbers of foreign students have been admitted …

- Use verbs (often with an impersonal subject) such as:
  hear, guess, imagine, suggest, suppose

- Use attitudinal signals such as:
  apparently, arguably, hypothetically, ideally, possibly, seemingly, superficially
  hopefully, strangely, unexpectedly, regrettably

- Use verbs such as:
  could, would, may, might

APPENDIX 5: WRITING ACADEMIC ESSAYS ON YOUR DEGREE COURSE

Suggested procedure

It is important to try to think in English throughout the stages of the writing process. Planning and writing in your first language and then translating will delay your progress in learning to write in English.

1. Brainstorm

When you feel you are ready to begin a writing task, make some quick notes about your ideas. Let your ideas 'flow' rapidly on paper, in any order. These can come in the form of words, diagrams, even visual images. Some interesting and unexpected associations of ideas can result from this effort. Try not to worry about the order or neatness of what you write. The aim is to achieve a rapid and spontaneous 'flow' of thoughts.

2. Plan your essay

(a) **Select** the most important and relevant points from your brainstorming.
(b) **Arrange** these in the most effective order.
(c) **Develop** further ideas if necessary.
(d) **Group** your points into coherent paragraphs, with each paragraph built around a single, unifying idea or topic.
(e) **Look for** gaps, repetition and irrelevant ideas.

Planning can be seen as a continuation of brainstorming rather than as a separate activity. Your essay plan can be done on a separate piece of paper if you wish or you can plan your essay by revising/rewriting your brainstorming on the same piece of paper. Arrows or numbers can be used to re-order and group your ideas.

   Refer again to the essay topic and make sure that what you have written answers it *fully* and *directly*. If you have any doubt about this, show your plan to another person in the same or a related subject area, and ask for critical comment (see point 4 below).

3. Write your first draft

At this stage it is best to concentrate on:

- content
- organisation
- cohesion
- vocabulary

The focus is on *what* you want to say and *how* you want to say it. A first draft is usually very rough and full of crossings-out, insertions, etc. Attention to grammar and mechanical accuracy can wait until a later stage in the writing process.

4. Evaluate and revise your first draft

With the aid of Evaluation Checklist B on page 29, improve and correct your draft. Refer to Sections 1 to 4 of the checklist for guidance at this stage.

5. Ask another person to evaluate your draft

Try to find a partner who is studying in the same or a related subject area – someone who does *not* speak your first language. Arrange a mutual exchange of drafts of essays with this person on a regular basis. Ask this person to make written comments and criticisms with reference to Sections 1 to 4 of Evaluation Checklist B. Then discuss these comments and decide whether or not you agree with them.

Repeated practice in the critical evaluation of another person's writing will make you a better critic of your own writing. As a result you should find your own writing improving more rapidly.

For two reasons it is important to find a partner who does not speak your first language. Firstly, you will continue the effort to think in English during the writing process, which in the long term will accelerate your progress. Secondly, a native speaker of your first language would be likely to make many of the same errors in language use and organisation that you will make and would probably find it difficult to recognise yours.

6. Make further revisions to your draft

Refer to Sections 5 and 6 of Evaluation Checklist B on page 29. Make corrections and improvements of this kind.

7. Write your second draft

By this stage, you will probably need to make only a few more changes as you write. These are likely to be minor ones. Clear handwriting is important at this point. Refer to any special instructions you may have been given about presentation – margins, double-spacing, etc.

Remember that some essays will need more than two drafts. Remember too that rewriting is not a sign of failure. The most essential difference between professional writers and other writers is that professional writers usually rewrite much more than other writers do.